Landscape Gardening

The Author

Dr. Sudhir Pradhan (born in 1958, M.Sc., Ph.D.) is a well known agri-journalist who has served DARE/ICAR for more than 3 decades in Government of India. The ICAR literature is now visible in more than 202 countries across the globe, and it has become possible through a project 'E- publishing and Knowledge System in Agricultural Research', an Indo- US Project (Among top 5 projects of the ICAR) under NAIP in which Dr Pradhan worked as Co-PI. In spite of short of man power the ICAR is having huge number of textbooks titles which became possible through 'Development of e-Publication system for Undergraduate/Postgraduate Textbooks' under Extramural Research Project, ICAR. Besides Dr Pradhan has more than 250 research and popular national and International standard articles, 1,000 news items, 20 books, 15 seminars, Book-Reviews, Radio & TV programmes. Editorial skilled-scientific work of the Council has involved Dr Pradhan has brought out several types of publications like Handbooks, Technical Books, Monographs, Technical Bulletins, Popular books, Reports like DARE/ICAR Annual Reports. Dr Pradhan has also served as expert consultations on thematic areas of high regional importance. Also he is instrumental in bringing out more than 40 issues of the ICAR Reporter, Indian Farming *etc.* from different countries in Asia Pacific region.

Landscape Gardening

Sudhir Pradhan

Union Ministry of Agriculture and Farmers Welfare-ICAR
New Delhi

BIOTECH

2021

BIOTECH BOOKS®

ISBN 978-81-7622-427-7

Published by: **BIOTECH BOOKS**®
4762-63/23, Ansari Road, Darya Ganj,
New Delhi - 110 002
Phone: +91-011-23262132
E-mail: biotechbooks@yahoo.co.in

Typeset at: **Classic Computer Services**
Delhi - 110 035

Digitally Printed at : **Replika Press Pvt. Ltd**

PRINTED IN INDIA

Preface

This book on Landscaping is meant to explain layouts of garden, informal gardens, formal gardens, shake gardens, vertical gardens roof gardens, paved gardens, bog gardens *etc.* The primary knowledge of gardening needs knowledge of climate and the way it affects shrubs, conditions of soil, and propagation and planting which is followed by principles of landscape design, gardening elements and design *etc.*

The delights of gardening with shrubs should appeal to everyone- whether for a small or large garden-for they are many. First, once a selection has been made, the position decided and planting correctly done, there is practically no further care required, beyond watering, feeding and, in a few cases, pruning. The shrub will from a permanent part of the garden, enduring for a lifetime. The value of the shrub as an individual thing of beauty, apart from its use in the landscape, lies also in the fact that it provides perennial and often unusual material for the vase. After all, on usually plans the garden around the house and it is a strange gardener who does not like to bring the prizes of the garden to add to the decoration of the house.

The layouts to grow shrubs and trees in this book were chosen with a certain number of ideas in mind. They have all been selected primarily for their intrinsic beauty. This applied to the beauty of the individual flower as well as to the showy effect that the flowers make on the bush as a whole. A few have been included because they fill a decorative place in the landscape, because of their shape or foliage, or have some other outstanding feature such as a sweet scent. Many shrubs and trees with arbitrary choice as no two people have exactly the same tastes. It is felt that the reader will probably come across some shrubs not included in this book that he might like to own, and will plant them at a later date, if possible.

The author has tried to choose design that are really desirable for the garden and grow easily and well in different parts of the country. As the gardener becomes more interest in shrubs he will want to possess many beautiful trait of the collector and applies as much to gardening as it does to collecting **objects d'art.** Many progressive nurserymen cater for these tastes; and many are the copper beeches and witch hazels that have been especially imported and grown very well in Arid conditions. But such shrubs and trees are rare and practically unobtainable here, so that they have not been included.

The book deals with 21 chapter namely, Etymology and Landscaping; Orchard planning, layout and Management; Climate and the way it affects the shrubs etc; the condition of soil; propagation and planting *etc.* I am sure that this title is useful to all garden lovers, students teachers, scientists, industrial personnel *etc.*

Dr. Sudhir Pradhan

Contents

Chapter 1

Etymology and Landscaping

There are several definitions of what constitutes a landscape, depending on context. In common usage however, a landscape refers either to all the visible features of an area of land (usually rural), often considered in terms of aesthetic appeal, or to a pictorial representation of an area of countryside, specifically within the genre of landscape. When people deliberately improve the aesthetic appearance of a piece of land–by changing contours and vegetation, *etc.*–it is said to have been landscaped though the result may not constitute a landscape according to some definitions.

Autumn Landscape.

The word 'landscape' (landscipe or landscaef) arrived in the United Kingdom–and therefore into the English language–after the Vth century, following the arrival of the Anglo Saxon: these terms referred to a system of human-made spaces on the land. The term landscape emerged around the turn of the XVIth century to denote a painting whose primary subject matter was natural scenery. *Land* (a word from Germanic origin) may be taken in its sense of something to which people belong (as in England being the land of the English). The suffix -scape is equivalent to the more common English suffix -ship. The roots of -ship are etymologically akin to Old English sceppan or scyppan, meaning to shape. The suffix -schaft is related to the verb schaffen, so that -ship and shape are also etymologically linked. The modern form of the word, with its connotations of scenery, appeared in the late XVIth century when the term landschape was introduced by Dutch painters who used it to refer to paintings of inland natural or rural scenery. The word landscape, first recorded in 1598, was borrowed from a Dutch painters' term. The popular conception of the landscape that is reflected in dictionaries conveys both a particular and a general meaning, the particular referring to an area of the Earth's surface and the general being that which can be seen by an observer.

Kukle, Czech Republic.

There are several words that are frequently associated with the word landscape:

- *Scenery*: The natural features of a landscape considered in terms of their appearance, esp. when picturesque: spectacular views of mountain scenery.
- *Setting*: In works of narrative (especially personified), it includes thehistorical moments in time and geographic location in which a story takes place, and helps initiate the main backdrop and mood for a story.
- *Picturesque*: The word literally means "in the manner of a picture; fit to be made into a picture", and used as early as 1703 (*Oxford English Dictionary*), and derived from an Italian term *pittoresco*, "in the manner of

a painter". Giplin's *Essay on Prints* (1768) defined picturesque as 'a term expressive of that peculiar kind of beauty, which is agreeable in a picture'.

- *A view*: 'A sight or prospect of some landscape or extended scene; an extent or area covered by the eye from one point'.
- *Wilderness*: An uncultivated, uninhabited, and inhospitable region.
- *Cityscape* (also townscape): The urban equivalent of a landscape. In the visual arts a cityscape (urban landscape) is an artistic representation, such as a painting, drawing,or print or photograph, of the physical aspects of a city or urban area.
- *Seascape*: A photograph or other work of art which depicts the sea, in other words an example of marine art.

Physical Landscape

Geo-morphology: The Physical Evolution of Landscape

Gemology is the scientific study of the origin and evolution of topographic and bathymetric features created by physical or chemical processes operating at or near Earth's surface. Geo-morphologists seek to understand why landscapes look the way they do, to understand landform history and dynamics and to predict changes through a combination of field observations, physical experiments and numerical modeling. Geo-morphology is practised within physical geography, geology, geodesy, engineering geology, archaeology and geotechnical engineering. This broad base of interests contributes to many research styles and interests within the field.

The surface of Earth is modified by a combination of surface processes that sculpt landscapes, and geologic processes that cause tectonic uplift and subsidence, and shape the coastal geography. Surface processes comprise the action of water, wind, ice fire, and living things on the surface of the earth, along with chemical reactions that form soils and alter material properties, the stability and rate of change of topography under the force of gravity, and other factors, such as (in the very recent past) human alteration of the landscape. Many of these factors are strongly mediated by climate. Geologic processes include the uplift of mountain ranges, the growth of volcanoes, isostatic changes in land surface elevation (sometimes in response to surface processes), and the formation of deep sedimentary basins where the surface of earth drops and is filled with material eroded from other parts of the landscape. The earth surface and its topography therefore are an intersection of climatic, hydrologic, and biologic action with geologic processes.

List of different Types of Landscape

Landscape Ecology

Landscape ecology is the science of studying and improving relationships between ecological processes in the environment and particular ecosystems. This is done within a variety of landscape scales, development spatial patterns, and organizational levels of research and policy.

How Past Volcanic Activity Shaped a Landscape.

Landscape is a central concept in landscape ecology. It is, however, defined in quite different ways. For example: Carl conceives of landscape not as a mental construct but as an objectively given 'organic entity', a "harmonic individuum of space". Errnst Neef defines landscapes as sections within the uninterrupted earth-wide inter-connection of geofactors which are defined as such on the basis of their uniformity in a specific land use, and are thus defined in an anthropocentric and relativistic way.

According to Richard Forman and Michael Gordan 'a landscape is a heterogeneous land area composed of a cluster of interacting ecosystems that is repeated in similar form throughout, whereby they list woods, meadows, marshes and villages as examples of a landscape's ecosystems, and state that a landscape is an area at least a few kilometres wide'.

Integrated Landscape Management

Integrated landscape management is a way of managing a landscape that brings together multiple stakeholders, who collaborate to integrate policy and practice for their different land use objectives, with the purpose of achieving sustainable landscapes. It recognizes that, for example, one river basin can supply water for towns and agriculture, timber and food crops for smallholders and industry, and habitat for biodiversity; the way in which each one of these sectors pursues its goals can have impacts on the others. The intention is to minimize conflict between these different land use objectives and ecosystem services. This approach draws on landscape ecology, as well as many related fields that also seek to integrate different land uses and users, such as water shade management. Proponents of integrated landscape management argue that it is well-suited to address complex global challenges, such as those that are the focus of the sustainable development goals. Integrated landscape management is increasingly taken up at the national, local and international level, for example the United Nations Environment Programme (UNEP) states that 'UNEP champions the landscape approach *de facto* as it embodies the main elements of integrated ecosystem management'.

Landscape Archaeology

Landscape archaeology or Landscape history is the study of the way in which humanity has changed the physical appearance of the environment - both present and past. Landscape generally refers to both natural environments and environments

Medieval Ridge and Furrow above Stanway.

constructed by human beings. Natural landscapes are considered to be environments that have not been altered by humans in any shape or form. The cultural landscapes, on the other hand, are environments that have been altered in some manner by people (including temporary structures and places, such as campsites, that are created by human beings). Among archaeologists, the term landscape can refer to the meanings and alterations people mark onto their surroundings. As such, landscape archaeology is often employed to study the human use of land over extensive periods of time. Landscape archaeology can be summed up by Nicole Branton's statement:' the landscapes in landscape archaeology may be as small as a single household or garden or as large as an empire, and although resource exploitation, class, and power are frequent topics of landscape archaeology, landscape approaches are concerned with spatial, not necessarily ecological or economic, relationships. While similar to settlement archaeology and ecological archaeology, landscape approaches model places and spaces as dynamic participants in past behavior, not merely setting (affecting human action), or artifact (affected by human action)'.

Cultural Landscape

The concept of cultural landscapes can be found in the European tradition of landscape design. From the XVIth century onwards, many European artists painted landscapes in favour of people, diminishing the people in their paintings to figures subsumed within broader, regionally specific landscapes.

The geographer Otto Schluter is credited with having first formally used 'cultural landscape' as an academic term in the early XXth century. In 1908, Schlüter argued that by defining geography as a Landschaft skunde (landscape science) this would give geography a logical subject matter shared by no other discipline. He defined two forms of landscape: the Urlandschaft (transl. original landscape) or landscape that existed before major human induced changes and the *Kulturlandschaft* (transl. 'cultural landscape') a landscape created by human culture. The major task of geography was to trace the changes in these two landscapes.

It was Carl O. Sauer, a human geographer, who was probably the most influential in promoting and developing the idea of cultural landscapes. Sauer was determined to stress the agency of culture as a force in shaping the visible features of the Earth's surface in delimited areas. Within his definition, the physical environment retains a central significance, as the medium with and through which human cultures act. His classic definition of a 'cultural landscape' reads as follows:

'The cultural landscape is fashioned from a natural landscape by a cultural group. Culture is the agent, the natural area is the medium, the cultural landscape is the result'.

A cultural landscape, as defined by the World Heritage Committee, is the 'cultural properties [that] represent the combined works of nature and of man.' The World Heritage Committee identifies three categories of cultural landscape, ranging from: (*i*) those landscapes most deliberately 'shaped' by people, through, (*ii*) full range of 'combined' works, to, (*iii*) those least evidently 'shaped' by people (yet highly valued). The three categories extracted from the Committee's Operational Guidelines, are as follows:

(*i*) 'A landscape designed and created intentionally by man';

(*ii*) An 'organically evolved landscape' which may be a 'relict or fossil) landscape'or a 'continuing landscape'; and

(*iii*) An 'associative cultural landscape' which may be valued because of the 'religious, artistic or cultural associations of the natural element'.

Human Conceptions and Representations of Landscape

Landscape Gardens

The Chinese garden is a landscape garden style which has evolved over three thousand years. It includes both the vast gardens of the Chinese emperors and members of the Imperial Family, built for pleasure and to impress, and the more intimate gardens created by scholars, poets, former government officials, soldiers and merchants, made for reflection and escape from the outside world. They create an idealized miniature landscape, which is meant to express the harmony that

Stourhead Garden, Wiltshire, England.

Jichang Garden in Wuxi.

should exist between man and nature. A typical Chinese garden is enclosed by walls and includes one or more ponds, scholar's rocks, trees and flowers, and an assortment of halls and pavilions within the garden, connected by winding paths and zig-zag galleries. By moving from structure to structure, visitors can view a series of carefully composed scenes, unrolling like a scroll of landscape paintings.

The English Landscape garden, also called English landscape park or simply the 'English garden', is a style of parkland garden intended to look as though it might be a natural landscape, although it may be very extensively re-arranged. It emerged in England in the early 18th century, and spread across Europe.The English garden presented an idealized view of nature. It drew inspiration from paintings of landscapes by Claude Lorraine and Nicolas Poussin, and from the classic Chineses gardens of the East, which had recently been described by European travellers and were realized in the Anglo-Chinese garden, and the philosophy of Jean – Jacques Roussea (1712 – 1778).

The English garden usually included a lake, sweeps of gently rolling lawns set against groves of trees, and recreations of classical temples, Gothic ruins, bridges, and other picturesque architecture, designed to recreate an idyllic pastoral landscape. The work of Lancelot 'Capability' Brown and Humphry Repton was particularly influential. By the end of the XVIIIth century the English garden was being imitated by the French landscape garden, and as far away as St. Petersburg, Russia, in Pavlovsk, the gardens of the future Emperor Paul. It also had a major influence on the form of the public parks and gardens which appeared around the world in the 19th century.

Landscape Architecture

The activities of a landscape architect can range from the creation of public parks and parkways to site planning for campuses and corporate office parks, from the design of residential estates to the design of civil infrastructure and the management of large wilderness areas or reclamation of degraded landscapes such as mines or landfills. Landscape architects work on all types of structures and external space – large or small, urban, sub-urban, and rural and with 'hard' (built) and 'soft' (planted) materials, while paying attention to ecological sustainability.

For the period before 1800, the history of landscape gardening (later called landscape architecture) is largely that of master planning and garden design for mansor houses, places and royal properties, religious complexes, and centers of government.

Central Park.

During the latter XIXth century, the term landscape architect became used by professional people who designed landscapes. Frederick Law Olmsted used the term 'landscape architecture' as a profession for the first time when designing Central Park, New York City, United States. Here the combination of traditional landscape gardening and the emerging field of city planning gave landscape architecture its unique focus.

Chapter 2

Orchard Planning, Layout and Management

Orchard planning and layout are which lays foundations of an orchard. The scientific planning and execution could result in optimum production, high returns and long orchard life. Proper planning includes evaluations of business goals, location, site characteristics, choice of crops, technical and management inputs, and market potential. Optimal site preparation and planting need to involve thinking in terms of managing tree roots for increased orchard performance at the first instance. Physical, chemical, and biological properties of the soil must all be considered as a holistic. A replant site necessarily requires two to three years of crop rotations in order to replenish organic matter, facilitate saplings establishment and avoid tree mortality or stunted growth. An ideal site needs to locate on the upper side of a gradual (4 to 8 percent) slope, on rolling or elevated land. Low lying areas, where cold air can accumulate during a calm, clear night, are prone to frost damage. Hilltops or ridges may expose trees to excessive winds or to arctic air masses. A southern-facing slope warms up faster in spring, while the opposite is true of a northern slope. Eastern-facing slopes are intermediate.

Selecting a site for an orchard about soil depth and soil texture. The deep (90 cm) and well drained soils are ideal for orchards. Soil analysis reports provides useful information on soil texture, parent material, native fertility, erosion levels, and water-holding capacity that are crucial. A well designed and comprehensive soil analysis considers such vital parameters as pH, EC, Organic carbon (C), Nitrogen (N), Phosphorus (P), Potassium (K), Calcium (Ca), Magnesium (Mg), Sulphur

(S), Iron (Fe), Manganese (Mn), Zinc (Zn), Copper (Cu), and Boron (B). Similarly analysis of water quality used for irrigation of orchard crops is also very crucial which normally considers parameters, pH, Electical conductivity (EC), Chloride (Cl), Nitrates (NO_3), Sulphates (SO_4), Carbonates (CO_3), Bicarbonates (HCO_3), Calcium, Magnesium, Sodium, RSC and SAR.

In normal as well as alkali soils, plants do not require liming; however, if the soil analysis shows lower pH than what is normally required (5.6-6.0) for wide range of fruit crops production, and in such instances agricultural lime should be applied and in case of magnesium (Mg) deficiency, dolomite should be used in order to amend the soil pH. If the soil is very acidic, heavy lime applications may be necessary based upon appraisal of the lime requirements. Two-thirds of the recommended quantity of lime need to be scattered over the area of planting mixed with the top soil, then the area ploughed as deep as possible and left at least 270 to 365 days before planting. Calcium (lime) moves very slowly downwards into the soil and must therefore be applied into the depth of the root zone. If a lighter agricultural lime application (2-4 tonne/ha) is required, the same could be applied into the soil at least 90 days before planting. It should only be applied when the pH is lower than the target soil (water) pH. In alkaline soils with a pH of 7-8, repeated applications of sulphur may be required at the rate of 500 kg/ha, until pH ranges from 5 to 6. In some problematic soils even after amendments, micro-nutrient deficiencies might occur that needs proper diagnosis and corrected accordingly by using appropriate foliar applications.

Before disturbing the surface vegetation, spot treatments could be made to control perennial and other problem weeds. On replant sites, a cover-cropping system needs to be established and maintained for several years in order to suppress weeds, nematodes, and soil-borne fungi and to increase soil organic matter. Soil drainage problems, if any should be corrected by establishing subsurface drainage systems or surface modifications such as ridging *etc.*, as some crops/rootstocks are especially sensitive to water-logging and associated diseases caused by *Phytophthora* species. There is a need to give considerable thought to the orchard design and tree quality. It is evident that branched trees on dwarfing rootstocks will produce early crops. To obtain the desired scion/rootstock combinations best suited to an orchard plan, it is important to ensure availability of quality trees well in advance at least a year ahead of planting. Planting of disease-free trees with healthy root systems ensures a good start for a sustainable production system. Well-hardened trees are desirable for early cropping and intensive systems. Windbreaks, if needed and pollinizers' trees also should be ordered early. Studies indicated that the best trees for windbreaks are casuarinas, Jack fruit', '*Jamun*' *etc.*, depending upon the location that are evergreen and leaf out early and also hold leaves throughout. Fruit tree bloom periods vary from one region to another, and it is advisable to get advice from the horticulture specialists on choice of pollinizers for different crops in order to augment productivity.

Trees planted in north-south oriented rows receive better light conditions than those grown in the east-west rows. Important considerations are canopy light interception and its distribution to flowers and fruit. Decreasing the distance between rows and increasing tree height also increases light interception. With most tree forms, the thumb rule is, optimum tree height works out to half the row spacing plus 90 cm. Maximizing production per unit area by planting trees in high densities requires careful assessment of the vigor potential of a site, use of a standard dwarfing rootstock and horticultural expertise. It may be helpful to evaluate tree size in a previous orchard or in an adjacent block before planning for such an effort. Other factors that affect decisions on tree arrangements include topography, equipment size, and worker access for critical cultural operations. The different components of orchard planning lay out and management are dealt in depth in the foregoing paragraphs.

Planning of an Orchard

Preparation of a blue print of orchard plan after taking into consideration different horticultural principles is necessary for ensuring the implementation good horticultural practices for optimizing production, sustained tree health, high orchard efficiency and profitability. While doing so, the following aspects are critical:

- ✰ Establishing site profile, outline decisions on soil amendments if required; green manuring and other approaches to improve soil fertility; site development by applying soil conservation and management principles, rain water harvesting and water conservation for efficient crop production.
- ✰ Location of different orchard structures like farm stores, office building, water resources should be centrally located for efficient supervision.
- ✰ It is important to allot each kind of fruit crop to a particular block in the field based fruits ripening time. Establishment of fence, wind breaks, roads order to ensure convenience.

Planting live fence with tall growing trees as first row and small, bushy thorny plants such as *Carissa carandas, Gliricidia sepium, Moringa,* Flame of the Forest, Palmyra palm, Babool, *Simarouba, Jamun, Jangal jalebi, etc.,* can also be planted as fence along the boundary of orchard. Some hedge plants make a thicker and denser fence by planting Agave, Sisal, *Boradi, Karonda* and *Mehandi etc.* In sloppy lands, planting of Vettiver grass helps in soil conservation.

Windbreaks

Tall trees are planted on the border of the orchard to reduce the impact of wind on the fruiting of trees. Trees suitable for windbreak should be erect, tall and quick growing, hardy and drought resistant and mechanically strong and having dense foliage and keeps the surrounding atmosphere humid and offer maximum resistance to wind. Trees, which are generally used as windbreak, are seedling mango, *jamun,* mulberry, moringa, jackfruit, carambola, shisham, teak, gamhar, bamboo, *Casuarina equisetifolia, Pterospermum acerifolium, Polyalthia longifolia, Eucalyptus globulus, Grevillea robusta, Azadirachta indica etc.*

In the planting pattern, special attention needs to be given for accommodating pollinizers varieties for different fruit crops. Normally it is advisable to see that every third tree in every third row is planted with pollinizers' variety.

Irrigation channels/facilities for laying out drip irrigation systems also need to be planned well in advance of planting.Roads should occupy minimum space for the economy of transport. Short growing trees should be allotted at the front and tall at the back for easy watching and to improve the appearance. Evergreen trees should be in the front and deciduous ones behind. Fruits attracting birds and animals should be close to the watchman's shed.

Establishment of Orchard

Establishment of an orchard is a long-term commitment of land requiring investment and hence deserves a thorough and critical planning exercise. The selection of proper location and site, site appraisal for suitability (soil profile and soil analysis; water resources development and water analysis), allotment of suitable crops, planting system and planting distance, choosing the varieties and the quality and disease- free nursery plants have to be carefully considered to ensure maximum orchard health and production.

Location and Choice of Site

Proper selection of site for orchard establishment is made based on the following criteria:

- The location should be in a well established fruit growing, near to the market.
- The suitable climatic conditions and free from weather vagaries.
- Availability of assured and adequate good quality water for irrigation.
- Fertile and well drained soils with good soil depth.

Preliminary Operations

The orchard site should be free from stumps or roots, shrubs and other. Deep ploughing is essential to remove big roots. The lands should be thoroughly ploughed, leveled and manured. In the hills, the land should be divided into terraces depending upon the slope.

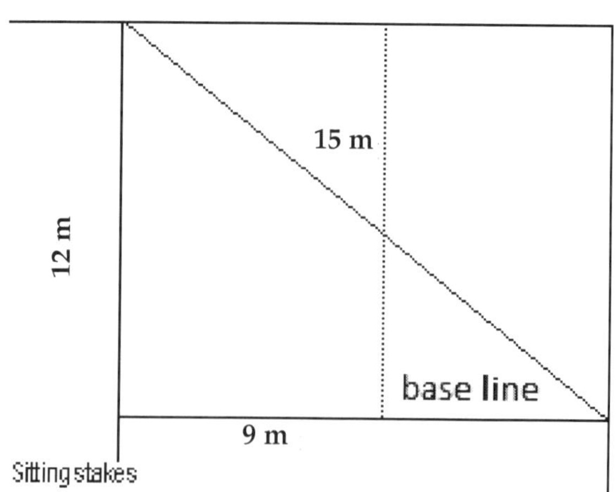

Lay out of an orchard on level land is a simple and is practiced through establishing a straight baseline, usually next to a fence or roadway. Then, lines at right angles to the baseline are established at both ends of the plot and one or two places in the middle. An easy way to establish these angles is to use three ropes whose lengths are in 3:4:5 proportions. Put the 4 m rope along the baseline, then place the 3 m rope at approximately a right angle, and finally, close the triangle with the 5 m rope.

Contour layout for sloppy land requires the use of a surveyor's level and rod. The first row is at the highest elevation, and is staked out on the level (*i.e.*, all points on the line are at the same elevation). Next, the steepest slope along the first row is found and the distance that has been selected as the minimum distance between rows is measured down the slope. From that point the next row is laid out on a level line as before. Moving away from this steepest slope to less-steep slopes, the rows will be wider apart. Wherever, the distance between two adjacent rows becomes twice the minimum distance, short contour row is laid out between them that point to the end of the plot. While planting litchi on contour, staggered method of planting is preferred between the two contours which utilizes the additional natural resources for production.

Any method of layout should aim at providing maximum number of trees per hectare, adequate space for proper development of the trees and ensuring convenience in orchard cultural practices. The system of layout can be grouped under two broad categories *viz.* (a) vertical row planting pattern, and (b) alternate row planting pattern. In the former planting pattern (*e.g.* square system, rectangular system), the trees set in a row is exactly perpendicular to those trees set in their adjacent rows. In the latter planting pattern (*i.e.* Hexagonal, Quincunx and Triangular), the trees in the adjacent rows are not exactly vertical instead the trees in the even rows are midway between those in the odd rows.

The different layout systems commonly adopted by the growers are detailed as below :

(a) Vertical Row Planting Pattern

Square System

In this system, trees are planted on each cornerer of a square. This is the most commonly followed system and is very easy to layout. The central place between

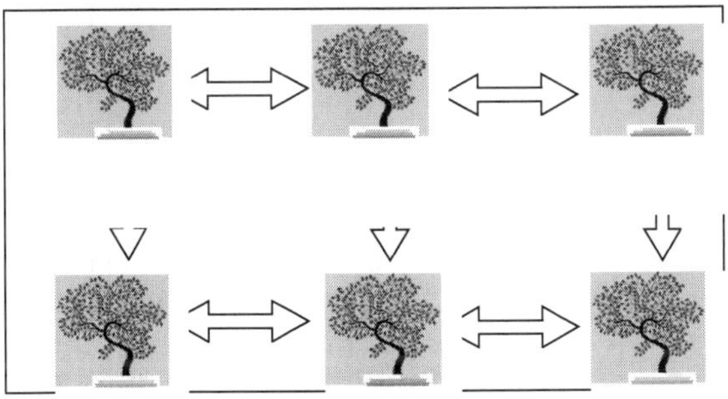

Square Planting.

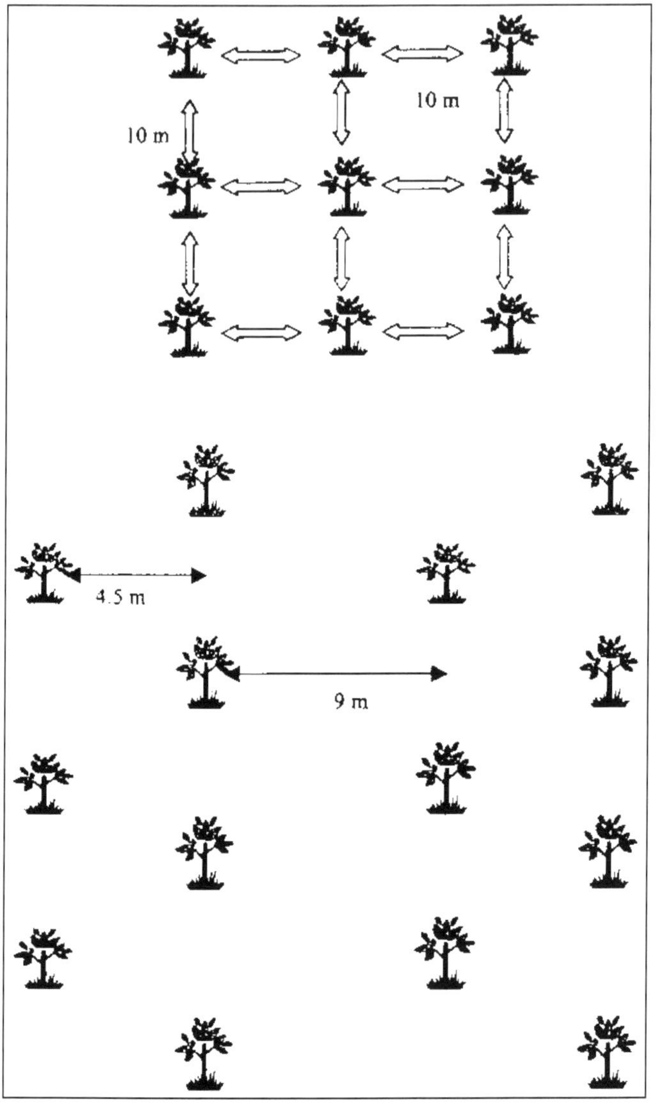

Plan of Orchards Showing Square System for Traditional Plantings (*Top*) and Double Gedgerow for Closer Plantings (*Bottom*).

four trees may be advantageously used to raise short lived filler trees. This system permits inter-cropping and cultivation in two directions.

Rectangular System

In this system, trees are planted on each corner of a rectangle. As the distance between any two rows is more than the distance between any two trees in a row, there is no equal distribution of space per tree. The wider alley spaces available between rows of trees permit easy intercultural operations and even the use of mechanical operations.

(b) Alternate Row Planting Pattern

Hexagonal System

In this method, the trees are planted in each cornerer of an equilateral triangle. This way six trees form a hexagon with the seventh tree in the centre. Therefore this system is also called as 'septuplet' as a seventh tree is accommodated in the centre of hexagon. This system provides equal spacing but it is difficult to layout. The perpendicular distance between any two adjacent rows is equal to the product of 0.866 x the distance between any two trees. As the perpendicular distance between any two rows is less than unity, this system accommodates 15 per cent more trees than the square system. The limitations of this system are that it is difficult to layout and the cultivation cannot be carried out so easily as in the square system.

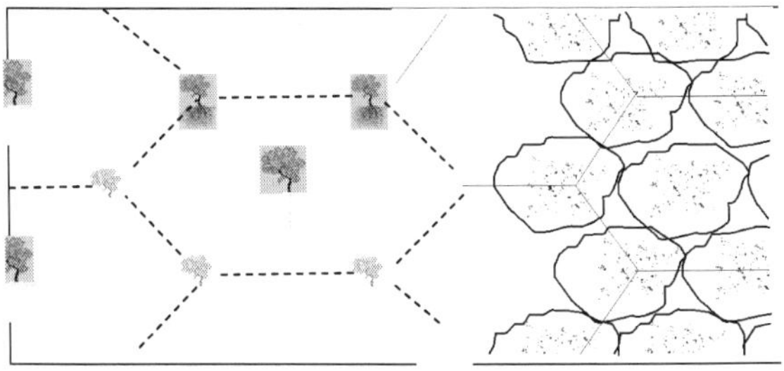

Diagonal or Quincunx System

This is the square method but with one more plant in the centre of the square. This will accommodate double the number of plants, but does not provide equal spacing. The central (filler) tree chosen may be a short lived one. This system can be followed when the distance between the permanent trees is more than 10 m. As there will be competition between permanent and filler trees, the filler trees should be removed after a few years when main trees come to bearing.

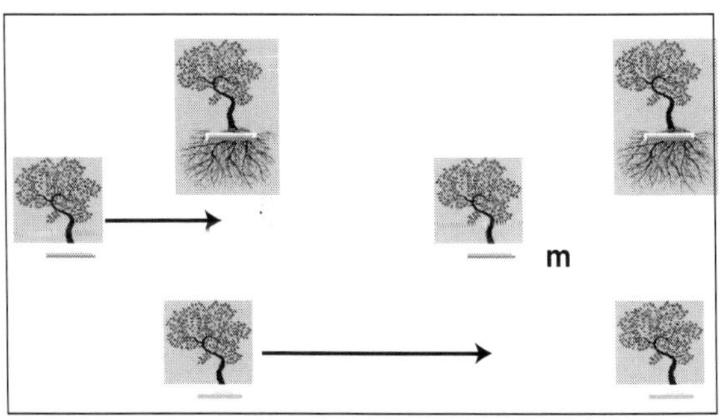

Triangular System

This is based on the principle of isolateral triangle. The distance between any two adjacent trees in a row is equal to the perpendicular distance between any two adjacent rows. However, the vertical distance, between immediate two trees in the adjacent rows, is equal to the product of (1.118 x distance between two trees in a row). When compared to square system, each tree occupies more area and hence it accommodates few trees per hectare than the square system.

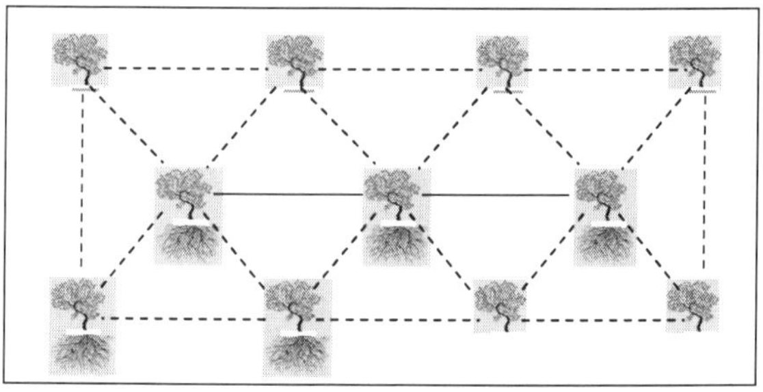

Triangular Planting

The Total Number of Trees per Hectare for some Important Fruit Crops Under (a) Square, (b) Hexagonal and (c) Triangular System of Planting

Crop	*Planting Distance (in m)*	*No. of Trees per Hectare*		
		Square System	*Hexagonal System*	*Triangular System*
Mango	10 x 10	100	115	89
Sapota	8 x 8	156	118	139
Clove	6 x 6	277	320	248
Acid lime	5 x 5	400	461	357
Guava	6 x 6	277	205	159

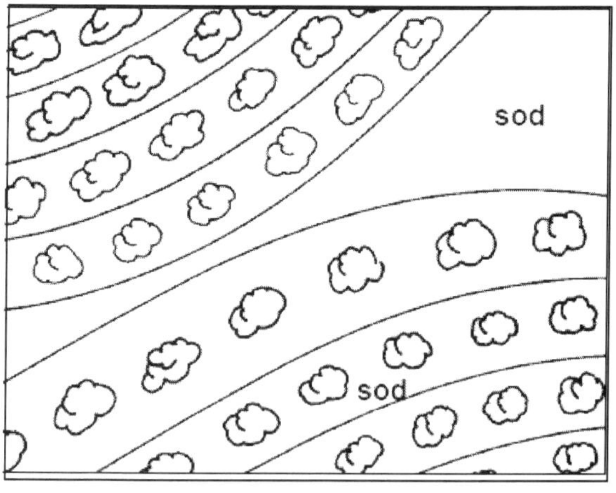

Contour Planting Using Parallel Rows or Terraces should be Used where Soil Erosion is a Problem.

Contour System

It is generally followed on the hills where the plants are planted along the contour across the slope following contour survey. The main purpose of this system is to minimize land erosion and to conserve soil moisture so as to make the slope fit for growing fruits and plantation crops. The contour line is so designed and graded in such a way that the flow of water in the irrigation channel becomes slow and thus finds time to penetrate into the, soil without causing erosion. Terrace system on the other hand refers to planting in flat strip of land formed across a sloping side of a hill, lying level along the contours. Terraced fields rise in steps one above the other and help to bring more area into productive use and also to prevent soil erosion. The width of the contour terrace varies according to the nature of the slope. If the slope becomes stiff, the width of terrace is narrower and *vice-versa*. The planting distance under the contour system may not be uniform. In South India, tea is planted in contours either in single hedge system or in double hedge system. Double hedge contour planting system accommodates nearly 22 per cent higher population than single hedge system. Number of plant population that can be accommodated in this system is:

$$\textbf{\textit{Plant Population}} = \frac{N \times \textit{Unit Area}}{D\,(y + z)}$$

where,

N: Number of hedges;

D: Distance between plants;

y: Distance between hedges;

z: Vertical distance between row

Single Hedge Row Planting

In this system, the plants are spaced closely in rows. The distance between trees in a row is usually one half one-third the distance between rows. This is practised only for high density plantings.

Double Hedge Row System

Digging of Pits.

The pits are dug one or two months prior to planting. The main purpose of digging and filling the pit is to provide congenial conditions for plant growth and development, especially during the establishment phase. The pits should be invariably opened during summer to expose the dug soil to heat and sunlight. Pits should be filled before the rainy season for proper settling of the loose soil. To prepare the pit certain steps need to be followed.

In light soils 60 × 60 × 60 cm planting pits are sufficient for litchi while in heavy soils 90 × 90 × 90 cm pits should be prepared. In *murrum* (gritty) soil, pit size may be increased up to 150 × 150 × 100 cm and 60-75 per cent of the dug soil is replaced with good soil and compost mixture. In locations, where the soil is loamy and deep, pits of 50 × 50 × 50 cm may be dug at desired distances. At hill slopes, the pits should be of 1 × 1 × 1 m size along the contour. At sloppy places, the pits are prepared in form of trench by cutting the upper side of slope and leveling the lower side of the slope. In this way a leveled platform is developed near the pit. Pit should be made in proper alignment so that saplings can be planted in the centre of the pit.

When the soil is taken out of the pit, the upper half soil is kept on one side and the lower half on other, under normal soil conditions; however, in *murrum* (gritty soil) the whole soil of pit is kept aside and top soil is filled. Dug out soil and open pit are left as such to weather for 2-4 weeks during summer to destroy any type of infection under sunlight and heat. In stony soils, it is better to separate all the stones from the excavated materials and left over soils should be mixed with manure and scrapped soil available in the field. Using a JCB machine for pit digging specially in hard and *murrum* soil is advisable because the pressure exerted by bucket of JCB cracks the hard pan which could allow the roots to penetrate.

Pit Filling

The pits are allowed to weather for few weeks before planting in some cases. The pits are then filled with top soil already mixed with red earth and well rotten farm yard manure. Irrigation is then applied to enable the contents of the pits to settle down properly. In the event of depressions taking place as a result of irrigation, more soil should be added to the pits to fill them to the level of the land. The pits are then ready for planting.

The pits should be filled with good quality substrate mainly include farmyard manure, de-oiled cakes, vermi-compost, *Trichoderma viride/Pseudomonas flourescens/Paecilomyces lilacinus* enriched rich manures and biofertilizers and vesicular arbuscular mycorrhizae culture. In rocky and *murrum* soils, which are almost zero in their inherent nutrient capacity, the initial substrate supplied in the pit governs the performance of the plant later. As a common dose, 30 to 40 kg *Trichoderma* enriched farmyard manure, 2 kg neem/*karanj* cake, 250 g single superphosphate or bone meal is sufficient for one pit in normal soil. In problematic soil however, pit soil should also be replaced with good soil. In highly acidic situation, application of 1-2 kg slaked lime, 250 g each of Zinc (Zn) and Boron (B) (Agriculture grade) is helpful to restore initial vigour of plant. Where magnesium deficiency is found to occur, 500 g dolomite should also be incorporated in pit filling mixture. Where soils are very sandy or infertile, the single super phosphate may be replaced by a 12-12-17 or similar type fertilizer mixture not less than two weeks prior to planting and, if possible, three-to-five months in advance. Fertilizers carefully mixed with topsoil should be placed at the bottom of the pit. If the soil is having infestation of white ants, fenvelerate/chloropyriphos dust is mixed with upper as well as lower soil of the pit. The upper soil of pit along with substrate is filled first followed by lower soil mixture. High quality soil mixture particularly the soil beneath the well grownup tree with probable Mycorrhiza (VAM) culture improves initial establishment and growth of saplings especially in crops like litchi, which is mycorrhiza (VAM) dependent. Similar is the case of citrus, of course in this case, the rootstocks themselves to be pre-colonized prior to budding. The main purpose of filling rich mixture in the bottom of the pit is that the plant will first proliferate their roots in 2/3rd lower portion of the pit. The upper level of pit is kept 15 cm above from the field level. After filling, if rain is not there, the pits should be irrigated to settle down the soil.

Planting Distance

Minimum vertical distance between any two fruit plants is referred as the planting distance and this varies depending upon different factors. The optimum planting distance is required for the most efficient and profitable use of land. Distance of planting is need based and dependent upon the nature and fertility level of soil;, cultivar vigour, growing conditions and purpose of orchard establishment. In poor soils, plants make slow growth, so require less space while in heavy soils, plant grow vigorously and therefore require more spacing.

Planting Methods

After locating the positions of the orchard trees, it is important that the trees are planted exactly where the stakes stood. It can be easily done with the help of a planting board. The planting board is placed in such a way that the stake (tree marker) fits into the central notch. A pit of about 1m cube or of the desired

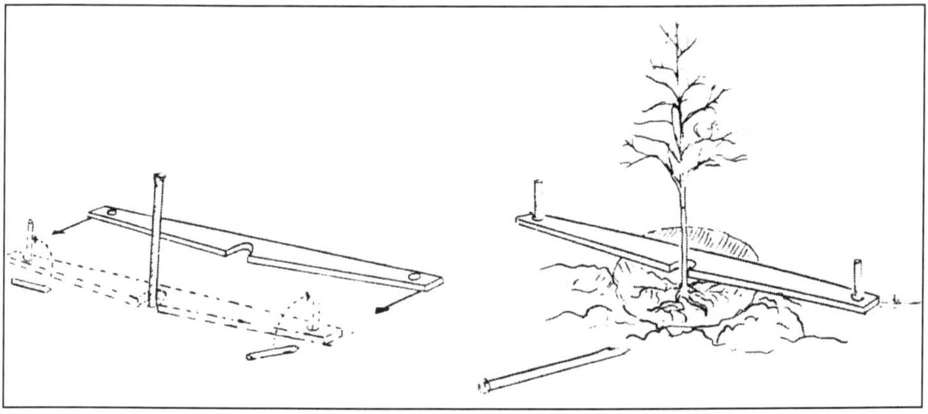

Use of Planting Board Helps in Setting Up a Plant at the Right Point during Planting Time while Establishing the Orchard.

Tree Guard and Staking

Newly planted trees should be provided with a tree guard of bamboo or wooden in a round or rectangle or square shape installed at the time of planting. It ensures protection from winds, bright sunlight and frost burn of main stem and branches.

Planting Season

The season of planting varies with different fruits and local conditions. There are two main seasons of planting in vogue in India, (*i*) Monsoon (June-August) and (*ii*) Spring (February-March). Monsoon is considered the best for planting evergreen fruit trees like citrus, mango, sapota and guava *etc.*, If the trees are planted early in the rainy season, they soon establish themselves and grow vigorously. Deciduous trees could be planted during the dormant period without shock. Care should be taken that planting is done before the growth starts, otherwise trees suffer severely and will be in poor condition to withstand the next hot weather.

Transplanting

The trees should be planted approximately where the original pegs had been placed. The trees are irrigated soon after planting.This consolidates the soil and. helps the roots to establish contact with it and to secure a supply of water quickly. A small basin may be made around the tree for this purpose. Planting if taken up during the rains, this basin should be demolished within a day or two so that water will not collect around the tree. This is more dangerous on heavy than light soils.

Soil Management Practices

Clean Culture

This type of cultivation is extensively followed in India. This involves regular ploughing and removal of weeds. The clean culture often has many disadvantages.

They are:

- ☆ Humus will be depleted rapidly due to frequent cultivation.
- ☆ Frequent cultivation causes injury to the feeding roots, the trees may be short lived or stunted in growth as it may facilitate entry of nematodes and pathogens.
- ☆ Clean cultivation aids in more aeration leading to the depletion of nitrogen. Hard pan is created in the soil.
- ☆ Frequent cultivation causes more soil erosion.

The above mentioned disadvantages in clean cultivation could be minimized by avoiding deep and frequent cultivation especially with heavy farm machinery and when the soil is too wet.

Clean Culture with Cover Crops

This type of soil management involves rising of a cover crop or green manure after removing the weeds. If clean cultivation is attempted during the rains, considerable erosion is almost sure to occur. It is probably best to plant a green manure crop between the trees early in the rains and plough it into the soil towards the end of monsoon season. In India, green manure crops like Sun hemp, Cowpea, Dhaincha, Lupines' *etc.* are more commonly used. Legume cover cropping in grape, mango, guava and other fruit crops is becoming a common practice in the management of orchards. Cowpea and French beans grow well under guava and sapota tree. In some places to prevent soil erosion, certain permanent cover crops like *Calapogonium muconoides, Centrosema pubescence* and *Peuraria phaseoloides* are raised in the alley spaces.

Mulching

This is one of the important soil management practices adopted in certain countries. Crop residues like straw, cotton stalks, leaves, saw dust, pine needles, coir dust arid other materials like polythene films or certain special kinds of paper are spread in the tree basins and in inter spaces between trees. Main objective of mulching is to conserve soil moisture, control the weed growth, keeps soil cool in day; warm at night hours, reduces surface run-off, adds humus to the soil, prevents soil erosion,.to keep fruits clean, and reduces irrigation frequency.

The following however, are some of the disadvantages:

(*i*) Dry materials used as mulches encourage the risk of fire and consequent damage to trees. In some soils, aggravate the incidents and buildup of termites.

(*ii*) Thick mulches may act as places for mice and rodents to live and multiply. They may cause damage to tree trunks and roots by eating the bark and burrowing to the land. The mulching materials should not be placed too close to the tree trunk and it should be spread in such a way that they give a good cover to the root system of the trees.

Intercropping

In young orchards, the question of how best one can use the soil in the interspaces of the trees arises. If the trees are properly spaced, there is considerable land available in the interspace of rows not being used by the permanent trees for several years. Similarly in the case of other long duration horticultural crops like tapioca, turmeric, ginger and banana some area between adjacent plants will be remaining unoccupied by the main crop for few months. It naturally appeals to the grower to get some returns from this vacant land especially when he is getting no returns in the early periods. The practice of growing any economic crop in alley spaces of the fruit trees in the first few years or in the unoccupied spaces of the long duration crop in the early periods is referred as intercropping. They also act as a cover crop and the land benefits by the cultivation, irrigation, manuring given to the intercrops.

The following important principles should be observed while growing intercrops.

(*i*) Intercrops should not occupy the area where the roots of the fruit trees are concentrated.

(*ii*) Soil fertility should be maintained or improved when intercrops are grown.

(*iii*) Water requirements of the intercrops should not clash with those of the main fruit trees. The intercrop may require irrigation at a time when it would be detrimental to the trees.

(*iv*) Intercrops should be selected with reference to their effects on soil moisture.

The Recommended Untercrops for some Important Horticultural Crops

Crop	*Age*	*Intercrop*
Mango	Up to 7 years	Leguminous vegetables, Papaya (filler)
Grapes	Up to 8 months	Snake gourd or bitter gourd in pendal
Apple, pears	Up to 5 years	Potato, Cabbage
Banana	Up to 4 months	Sun hemp, onion, ginger, turmeric, Colocasia
Tapioca	Up to 3 months	Onion, beans, lab-lab, black gram
Turmeric	Up to 3 months	Small onion, coriander
Areca nut	Up to 10 years	Pineapple, Cocoa, Black pepper, Banana
Coconut	Up to 3 years	Banana, tapioca, vegetables

Mixed Cropping

It refers to the practice of growing certain perennial crops in the alley spaces of the main perennial crops. The main advantage here is the effective utilization of available area and increases the net incomes of the grower from unit area. Extensive research conducted by CPCRI, Kasaragod on mixed cropping in coconut and areca nut plantations showed that cocoa, pepper, cinnamon, clove and nutmeg could be grown as mixed crops in coconuts while, nutmeg and clove as mixed crops in between four areca nut palms on alternate rows. In all the above cases, increase in yields (up to 10 per cent) is obtained in the main crop due to the synergistic effects of the crop combinations arising out of the beneficial micro-organisms in the rhizosphere and increased availability of major nutrients in the active root zone of the crop mix as compared to the pure stands.

Multitier System of Cropping

Certain horticultural crops like coconut and areca nut are grown for about 50 years or so in a particular land. It normally takes 4 to 7 years for these trees to reach the bearing stage. Adequate alley spaces (nearly 75 per cent) are available in between these trees and being the palm trees, their root system would not have extended beyond one meter in diameter. Hence, the available vacant spaces could be profitably used for raising other crops, thereby increasing the employment opportunities and profits to the grower. Intercropping and mixed cropping involve jointly multitier system of cropping and is defined as compatible companion of crops having varying morphological frames, rooting habits and with diverse natural resources' mining potential, grown together in such a manner that their canopies intercept solar energy at varying heights while their roots explore the soil at different zones for water and nutrients. The main principle is that the land, water and sunlight should be effectively used. An ideal combination of crops for multitier cropping in coconut and areca nut plantations is as follows:

Tier	*Crop*
First (Top)	Coconut or areca nut
Second	Pepper trained over the trunk of coconut or areca nut trees
Third	Cocoa or cloves planted at the centre of four areca nut or coconut
Fourth (ground)	Pineapple, ginger and dwarf coffee

Water Management

Efficient orcharding, to a great extent depends upon optimum use of water especially during critical stages of plant growth and development. *'More crops/per drop'* is the approach now. Main sources of irrigation are either open wells or bore wells with pipelines laid out along the gradient connecting various blocks preferably availing the expertise of a water management specialist. Necessary care is required to avoid water logging. Addition of silt, clay, organic matter *etc.*, increases field capacity and also raises wilting point to marginal increase. Rainwater harvesting (RWH) for utilization later for different situations has become a dire necessity in the emerging context of water becoming a scarce resource input. The same under *in situ* orchard conditions which is crucial especially for dry land orcharding could be optimized through different ways.

Organic Farming

Excessive use of chemical fertilizers and pesticides as a mean of intensive cultivation to boost up our food production has caused considerable damages to the soil health and the environment. This has been criticized recently by many environmentalists. This has focused the attention of several experts in ecologically sound viable and sustainable farming systems, known as organic farming. It is a production system which avoids or largely excludes the use of synthetically compounded inorganic chemicals. This system entirely relies on crop rotation, crop residues, animal manures, legumes, green manures, off-farm organic wastes, biofertilizers, mechanical cultivation *etc.* and aspects of biological pest control to maintain soil productivity and tilth to supply nutrients and to control insects, weeds and other pests. This system is often, referred as 'biological farming' 'regenerative farming' and 'sustainable farming' 'ecofriendly farming' *etc.*

Chapter 3

Climate and the Way its Affects the Shrubs

If there are four types of climates such as temperature, winterfall, arid and rainfall it follows that many shrub will be found growing vigorously in parts of the country which will not survive in others. This applies to indigenous shrubs, meaning those found growing wild in the country, as well as to those imported shrubs which started life in China, Japan, United Kingdom and United States of America and have been grown all over the world without many people knowing or caring about the country of their origin. This fact really concerns only the botanist or naturalist, but it is also valuable to the average gardener in so far as it gives a clue on how to treat each shrub, by trying to imitate condition found in its natural home and so giving it an opportunity to flourish in any garden anywhere in the world.

There are a number of basic differences in climate which make it difficult for shrub and trees to survive where they do not have what they need. Temperature, moisture and light are the three most important influences in the life of a plant. Soil conditions are important too, but do not hold first place and do not come in at this stage while we are discussing climate. When considering temperature, we must note whether the plant is used to a hot climate or a cold, and whether too much of either extreme will affect it in such a way that it will not be able to survive. This is where the all-important question of frost crops up. A tender shrub, such as Poinsettia, which thrives in warm Natal, will not survive the frost of the Highveld, even if it has grown vigorously all the year round, unless the gardener takes some precaution in giving it a sheltered spot where the frost will not kill it altogether. In this case, therefore, it is possible to take a plant from the sub-tropical climate and grow it successfully in the frost area, provided that one knows the weakness of the plant that tends to succumb to cold and protects it accordingly.

Light plays an important part in the life of many plants. Numbers of shrub can be planted anywhere in the garden but there are many that will thrive best in the shade, such as Fuchsia, and those that will do well only in the open sun, such as Erythrina. Naturally the exceptions can always be found, but on the whole one gets the best results if one knows which are the shade-loving shrub and plants them in the shade and *vice versa*. This knowledge also helps in planning the garden, when one can make a point of placing shade-loving plants under the shade of trees and can make them a feature of the landscape.

Moisture is the third important element to be considered. In a generally arid country, this might almost be all-important, but it is possible to give certain shrub too much moisture. Sometimes this point is over-done and people warm the amateur gardener about the dreadful result of overwatering, such as mildew and rot. Unfortunately, most gardeners under- water in any case, so that these sad results are seldom evident. In annual plants, over watering can wreak havoc, but the beauty of growing shrubs is that they can take overwatering very well and revel in it. One has only to see the growth put on by many shrub and trees can survive with very little water, as they are used to thirst in this parched land of even they respond to cultivation and good watering, and outstrip their veld sisters in size and flowering.

This discussion on the climatic requirements of shrubs, does not mean that it is only possible to grow those which do well in your own area. Besides, as one becomes more and interested in gardening, it is inevitable that one will want to grow those shrubs which do not do well in one's own area, but come from differen provinces and are rare in one's own home town. The old story of forbidden fruit holds good and it becomes much more exciting to grow a tender, rust-coloured Bougainvillea that might not survive the winter in a cold area than the ordinary hardy purple Bougainvillea that spreads in a wealth of colour in the summer.

It is not necessary to go the extreme of the old French gardener, and one should definitely grow those shrubs which do well in your area as well as those which need particular requirements. The gardener must first know what those special requirements are and then do his best to provide them. It is certainly easy to plant a shade-loving shrub in the shade, whether complete shade or filtered sunlight, under a tree such as a Syringa. Other shrubs that do not care particularly for shade can be planted anywhere in the open sun of the garden. Moisture too, can be controlled to a large extent. In the dry winter of the Transvaal, a shrub that comes from the winter rainfall area of the Cape should be well watered so as to simulate the shrub's natural home or habitat. Humidity plays an important part in the amount of moisture available. Hydrangeas are usually grown in the shade in the Transvaal and given a great deal of water during the summer months. In Durban and Cape Town, however, the humidity of the atmosphere near the sea keeps the fleshy leaves turgid and does not allow rapid transpiration or loss of moisture through the leaves, so that one often sees Hydrangeas growing right out in the open sun without wilting, as they would do in a dry atmosphere. In dry areas on a very hot day, it often helps to spray plants such as Hydrangeas and Azaleas with the hosepipe to retard transpiration from the leaves, which may or may not show signs of wilting. Proper watering makes it possible for shrubs to grow even in the semi-desert areas, provided that one can obtain the water for gardening.

One of the biggest enemies of moisture is the wind, for this dries the leaves rapidly so that they lose more moisture by evaporation than can absorb through their system from their roots. The consequence is that the leaves, not having enough moisture in them, become wilted, and the plant will suffer if this not remedied, as the leaves are the breathings of plant, converting the sunlight and air into nourishment. In windy weather, therefore, the gardener should pay extra attention to the watering of shrubs, particularly if it also hot at the same time. Here again it helps to spray the leaves. In the case of shrubs that dislike wind, see that they are protected from the wind by other shrub, trees or even a well.

The battle against frost, however, is not so easy. One can try to prevent the ravages of frost, but this cannot be as easy as controlling the requirements of light and moisture. Frost comes in winter, through not every winter, to the gardens of the Highveld. It does not come to Natal or the Cape as a rule, unless the altitude is very high.

Normally there is a very short period of frost, which comes for a few nights, but this is enough to cause the death of many tender plants, unless they are protected. Frost accompanied by wind is called a 'black frost', so called beyond all chance of recovery. In the case of particularly tender shrubs, they whole shrub is affected and cannot recovery, but in many cases, after the blackened parts are cut away, the shrub will send out new growths in the spring. Each year, unless there is no frost, the cycle will be repeated, so that one need not lose the shrub completely. Also, a slight frost might not affect them, whereas a hard frost would. Such shrubs can be called 'half-hardly'. A 'hardly' shrub, on the other hand is that will endure the hardest frost and is the gardener's joy, particularly on the Highveld. 'Tender' shrubs are so-called because they cannot endure frost, although no strict rules can be laid down as to whether these will be completely annihilated by frost or merely have their tender young growth affected.

The gardener can Plant shrub in special position in order to protect them the frost, by finding warm spots for those plants which come from a hot climate. In arid climate, a north-facing wall is the warmest spot in winter, and one should try to plant all very tender shrubs in front of a north-facing wall, hedge or even a clump of other hardier shrubs.

One must really understand what frost is, before realising why simply facing north is not always good enough. When a after the frost or dew has settled, which thaws the cold frost off and in so doing burns the tender growth, much in the same way as a human being gets frost-bite if he places his frozen hand into hot water or near a fire. So we can understand why it is necessary to protect the tender shrub from the morning sun. The shrub should have shade in the early morning so that the frost can thaw slowly by itself, and receive the sun at mid-day and in afternoon to give it heat once more. In other words, a tender shrub should not be placed facing east if possible. Hibiscus, for example, will do better if it is placed in a corner against the house where one wall faces north and the other west, than if it is merely placed facing due north and receives the early morning sun. Even a position simply facing west is preferable to that facing east, but here there should be some protection from cold south winds if the shrub is to do well.

Walls retain the heat of the sun and that is why they are the warmest spot for some tender shrubs, but other (such as petrea), although they like warmth, prefer a position where there is more circulation of air than is found against a wall. Protect nooks can be found or made in any garden. A section of the garden, about 6 or 9 m long, can be a sheltered spot if it has a screen of trees or shrubs on its south side and a few hardly shrubs east and west, roughly forming the three sides of a box. A split pole fence overgrown with creepers, or a low garden wall, can also from one of the sides of this rough 'box', which should certainly not be too symmetrical, for appearance sake.

A popular method of protection against frost is 'covering' the shrubs for the winter. The danger here is that many shrubs are often suffocated and die from lack of air instead of from the frost. This usually happens when the unfortunate shrubs are swaddled in hessian, which is tied right up against the body of the plant, so that there is no circulation of air. The best material for covering them. This is the long veld grass which is already dry and brownish and should be cut off as long possible (it is usually four to five feet long).

A framework of pliable, bared twigs should be made first around each shrub. The branches of the Wattle tree are very suitable and stakes should be cut off to the required length with all leaves removed. Placed four of five stakes around each shrub, which, when tied together at the top are at least one foot higher than the tip of the shrub. Then tie two or three horizontal rows of pliable twigs on to these stakes, so that the framework crudely resemble the framework of a red-Indian tent. The long grass is stacked in bundles against this framework and tied right around with several pieces of string. Leave air-spaces here and there, particularly on the western side of the 'tent'. The grass will meet at the top and prevent the frost from setting on the shrub. This covering should be put on at the beginning of winter and left until all danger of frost has passed. It permits a free circulation of air around the shrub, without which it cannot live. Watering should continues as before.

It is fact that a shrub which has been planted in the open and has been covered in this way for the first four or five winters, will finally grow very big and strong and be so well established that it is unnecessary, and even inconvenient, to continue with the covering. At most, only the new young grow will be affected by a frost and this can be trimmed off without further effects. It is for the gardener to judge the vigour and size of his shrub and decide when to stop covering in winter.

In spite of all these precautions against frost, however, losses often occur, so that frost remains the great leveler, and whether the shrub is tender to frost or frost or not, is the most important thing to consider when choosing new shrubs for a garden which is situated in an area where heavy frost falls in winter.

It can be seen, therefore, that any shrub can be tried or planted anywhere in arid climate, provided that one learnsin advance what are the ideal requirements for each shrub and it willing to provide them to the best of one's ability. This sort of knowledge prevents many disappointments on the part of the average gardener. It prevents the disappointment of loss when a shade-loving plant cannot survive in a sunny spot, a moisture-loving plant does not thrive in a dry spot or when a favourite tender shrub is lost during winter simply because it had no protection. The hardiest sun-loving shrub which can survive the coldest winter, will also prove a disappointment to the gardener if it is planted in a shady spot. Even though it will live and grow, it will do neither vigorously, and the beauty of its flowering will be spoiled, so that the gardener will take a dislike to it and think that it was not a good shrub to have grown. Half an hour spent in locating a good position for each shrub will be rewarded with extra weeks of attractive flowering each years and a healthy bush which forms an indispensable part of the landscape.

On the other hand, the gardener need not be too discouraged by this task, as shrubs, like human beings, can withstand a great deal of buffeting and will survive many risks. It is often the neglected fig tree behind the servant's quarters that bears the most abundant figs.

The best way to ensure that delicate and 'difficult' shrubs will do well in your area is to grow them from seed. If they grow up knowing no other climate, than they will acclimatize themselves and adjust themselves gradually, in the same way as the skin adjust itself to the sun and assumes an even than if it is exposed gradually. Some shrubs, such as Bauhinia, grow very easily and rapidly from seed, but infinite time and patience or is willing to take cuttings.

When buying shrubs in tins try, as far as possible, to buy from a nursery near by, so that your own climatic conditions will resemble those to which the plant is accustomed.

Within the area of one's own garden there are different little pockets of climate. This may be seen when two similar trees planted a little distance away from each other, often grow unevenly. The gardener different climatic conditions, and decide for himself which are the warm, cool, protected or exposed positions in his own garden. This enable him to grow a large variety of shrubs which will respond to suitable conditions with healthy, vigorous growth and abundant flowers.

Chapter 4

The Condition of the Soil

The condition of the soil is of the utmost importance of and trees are to be grow, successfully. The wrong type of soil will never good results, but it is very to create the right type of soil. The idea thing would be for the gardener to prepare a large piece of ground and improve all the ground and its drainage, but this is not always practicable. The gardener, however, can do a great deal for his shrubs by simply changing the soil in the small area which each shrub will occupy.

Good garden soil is recognized as having a rich, dark brown colour and a soft crumbly texture, which has neither too much clay to make it stiff nor sand it poor. It can be presumed that such a soil is fairly rich in organic matter, particularly if there are earthworms present, since they exist only in a soil which contains organic matter. In time, they future improve the soil by consuming it and passing it out of their bodies in the from of worm casts. These casts are rich in food value and have a fine texture. The earthworm also aerates the soil by borrowing through the earth, as deeply as five to six feet, and lining these burrows with a substance rich in plant foods.

The aim is to supply a good garden soil which is a copy of the fertile soil in which the shrubs grow in their wild state. Fertile soil is rich in organic matter such as leaves and manures which have accumulated and decomposed over the centuries. Man's imitation of this is the manufacture of compost and the addition of this to the soil. Not only is it possible to increase the fertility of the soil by the use of manure and compost, but there is another requirement in the soil to be considered, which varies with the different shrubs, and is known as the acid reaction of the soil. Both of these essentials must be discussed in detail, for the gardener is able to change his to suit his shrubs, provided that he is acquainted with what they want.

Manure or Compost?

The question is often asked, "Why use manure if compost can supply all that is required in the soil?" the fect is that compost should really contain manure, for in uncultivated land the manure dropped by wild animals become part of the humus formed by decomposing leaves. It is important to use both compost and manure, for each plays a very definite part in both gardening and farming.

Recently, a natural phenomenon known as mycorrhizal association has been studied in England by Dr M C Rayner,who has written pamphlets and book and carried out numerous experiment on the subject, and her findings throw a new light on importance of compost.*

Myco mean 'fungal' and rhiza means 'root'. Growing trees have been found to have a fungus growing at the which inter-connects he soil and the growing system of the tree. This is not a parasitic fungus, but one that plays an important part in the life of the tree. *Mycorrhiza* is the name used to describe the tree root plus its thread-like fungi or *mycelium.* It is agreed that soil fungi break down complex substances that are otherwise not available to shrubs and trees and that they also excrete substances that stimulate growth. *Mycorrhizal* association suggests that many plants benefit from *specific* Soil fungi. Dr. Rayner proves that in some cases (HEATHS or ORCHIDS) normal seedling development depends on the presence of the fungus, or growth can be stopped without it. Now vigorous fungal activity is dependent on a sufficient supply of humus or compost, and the fungi cannot live in soil without it, so that the addition of compost is of paramount importance when planting a tree or shrub.

Compost does not act directly by supplying nourishment in itself, but it acts indirectly by stimulating the activity of the soil fungi. The action of these fungi, in association with the tree roots, stimulate growth in a remarkable way, surpassing result obtained by using inorganic chemicals, and in addition improving the health and strength of the tree and its powers of resisting disease. Also, shrubs growing on compost-treated soil are more likely to survive hard winters. Compost is therefore essential when planting shrubs and trees, particularly indigenous specimens, as much as possible of the soil in the area in which the tree has been growing should be taken with it, and a good "ball" of earth should be taken. Compost also improves the texture of the soil. A stiff clay will be made porous and a sandy soil held together by the addition of compost.

Manure supplies nutrients to the roots direct. When planting a shrub, it is customary to add manure to the lower half of the hole which is prepared for it, so that, after a season, when the shrub has established itself, its reach the now very well–rotted manure and grow vigorously. Manure is not only a food but a stimulant, and the shrub seems to spring forward in growth when its roots reach it, deep down. There are those who say that it is unnecessary to add manure to the subsoil since it has been proved that only the top six inches of the soil contains the mass of organic matter and the bacteria which are essential to plant life. As one digs lower, the bacteria decrease considerably. This is true, but from the gardener's point of view it is highly desirable to improve the subsoil. The gardener who gets a thrill out of seeing his shrubs do well will find it a pleasure to do something practical to hasten the best results. It seems obvious that one should try and improve the subsoil as the top-soil when planting a shrub for permanent enjoyment in the garden, reather than leave the subsoil in its original state of unfriendly hardness. Then, too there is the question of drainage to be provided at the bottom of the hole, so that while one is in the process of digging out the subsoil, one should add the manure which will later be of benefit to the shrub.

Compost

Compost is composed of decayed plant material, and there is no doubt that its addition to the soil works wonders. The case for compost is unopposed, and the only question that occupies gardeners is that of how the compost should be made. There have been books written on the subject of compost, which is a complete study in itself, and there are many theories and methods of making it which have been and are being perfected by experts.

The main thing is that the gardner should have a continous supply of compost all the year rond. Every time he wants to plant a shrub, there should be a fresh supply on hand, and this can also be used as a top dressing around one's shrubs as well as all over the garden. Compost must be properly made if it is to do its work successfully, and should include some product of animal origin since compost does not nourish the plant direct but stimulates the fungi in the soil.

Briefly, these are the methods used in making compost. The old, enormous pit, which is now outmoded as a means of making compost, was a convenient dump for rubbish but had many disadvantages. In addition to the many months one had to wait for compost, there was usually a bad smell from these pits as the vegetable matter was putrefying and not decomposing correctly. Also, there was no air for the bacteria which bring about the decomposition of the compost.

There are three popular methods of making compost, two above ground and one below the surface. When making compost above ground, one may build heaps or make the compost with the aid of a box or frame. Here the living organisms which break down the vegetable matter are able to breathe. The decomposition creates heat which should be kept in by use of earth or sacks, which also help to keep out excess moisture such as storm-water, which might exclude the air by saturation.

Any heap that is well made will eventually turn into good compost, but it has been found that the addition of activators will speed up the whole process of making compost in quite a remarkable way (by stimulating or activating the micro-organisms).

Fresh manure is the ideal land natural activator and other organic activators are drief blood, sewage sludge, papaw pips crushed with water and untreated tobacco dust or leaves. Commercial activators are sold by seedsmen and are very good if they aremade up of organic material. Experiments in England tend to prove that although chemical activators rot the vegetable matter quickly, organic matter used a an activator produces a greater degree of disease resistance in plants. Apart from this consideration, animal residues such as farmyard manure, dried blood or sewage sludge should be include in compost, since the fungi in the soil feed on compost and require a mixed diet of animal and vegetable matter.

The details of building up the compost are the same whether you make an open heap or build it up in a frame or box.

The heaps are about five feet square and three to four feet high. The heat will evaporate too readily from smaller heaps and large ones are too difficult to handle. The boxes or frames vary in size from two feet square to six feet square according to one's need and are made of planks or split poles on four sides but not at the bottom. They have rmovable from and are covered by a lid or sack.

In both cases the material are added in layers, starting with a six-inch layer of green matter, followed by a two-inch layer of manure and then a thin covering of good soil. A sprinkling of agricultural lime is then added and then another six-inch layer of green matter. The layers are built up in this way to the desired height.

While building the heap, two or more stake should be placed upright near the centre so that when the layers are completed, these may by withdrawn to provide air vents. Ready prepared activators are usually poured in solution down these holes. Cover the last layer with soil and then with sacks in order to keep the heat in. the finished heap should be watered but not saturated. The heaps should be turned over twice, at intervals of about a month, so that every part of the compost has a chance of being in the centre where the greatest heat is concentrated.

Making compost in bins or heaps is very successful in those parts of the country which have a most atmostphere such as at the coast, but in dry atmospheres it is very difficult for the gardener to keep the heaps in the ideal state of moisture. Exposed as they are to the air, they will dry out rapidly and thus slow down the whole process, so that one should use these methods only when conditions of humidity prevail.

In the dry atmosphere of the Transvaal, there is yet another method of making compost which has been used with great success. It is easy to prepare, maintain and handle, and can be used in the small garden as well as on large estates. This method also ensures a continuous supply of compost.

Three shallow pits are dug side. They are each 18 deep and about four feet square. The green matter is put into the first pit, together with the manure or other activator, soil and a sprinkling of lime. Make several layers and allow the top to protrude slightly above the ground as it will ink down while decomposing. Water it and cover with soil or sacks. After three weeks, throw it all into the second pit, and after another three weeks, throw it into the third. At the same time recommence the process in the first pit. At the end of about ten weeks you will have excellent compost, and if you follow up the routine in the other two pits, you will have a continuous supply throughout the year. The compost should be sifted before using, and the residue put back into the first pit.

This is a good method since it enables you to use the garden rubbish as it accumulates continuously. It is also easy and inexpensive and requires very little labour, for the smallness of the pits make the compost easy to handle when throwing it from one pit to the other, a task which turns it at the same time. It seems to be the common-sense method which would appeal to all gardeners. All compost should be used as soon as possible after it is ready.

Soil

Soils are of two types (*i*) acidic and (*ii*) alkaline.

Acidic and Alkalinity of the Soil

It sometimes happens that despite a carefully chosen position, as well as adequate feeding and watering, a shrub will not thrive. It may start off by simply not flowering, and later die back slowly. This is often a grat puzzle to the gardener. Many a gardener has bought a beautiful flowering AZALEA and found to his great disappointment that the following year masses of promising looking buds will turn brown and wither, so that not a single flower will be produced. After a year or two of watering carefully, not too much and not too little, without success, he gives up and imagines that AZALEAS are difficult.

What is the "mystery" that makes them do well in some gardens? Is it the "green-finger" of the gardener who has some secret handed down from generation to generation? Very often this mystery of the soil can be solved very scientifically in the study of the acidity and alkalinity of the soil.

This need not be as difficult or complicated as it sounds because modern research supplies the answer quite easily. A sample of your soil can be sent to any Agricultural College or Government Agricultural department and they will give you a report on your soil. Any analytical chemist will also be able to supply the same information and there are also very simple soil-testing kits from America which are available to gardeners.

It is necessary to understand what the report means in scientific terms. The degree of acidity or alkalinity is referred to as the pH value of the soil. For a neutral soil the pH is 7. Numbers from 7 to 14 indicate the degree of alkalinity and number 7 back to 0 indicate the degree of acidity of the soil. Research stations determine the exact pH preferences of each plan or shrub, and special plant lists are made and given by soil-testing laboratories.

The exact pH preferences need not be followed strictly by amateur gardener, but they do give an idea of the requirements of the different plants and can consulted for accuracy where plants are not doing well. In other words, the reaction of the soil is of the greatest importance and the modern gardener should consider the pH preference of his shrub in the same way as he considers the positions in which they are to be planted. Also, in he same way that the gardener improves the fertility of poor soil with compost and manure, so can make a soil more acid or more alkaline.

It is easy to make a soil more alkaline or "sweeter" by agricultural lime. One simply sprinkles it over the surface of the ground, lightly forking it in and following by a good watering.

In South Africa one always hears the saying is sour (acid) and can never have too much sweetness –in the form of lime. Lime assists in making available more readily the essential ingredients of the soil, but if the soil is over-limed, as it is when the pH of the soil is raised above8, then these essential mineral nutrients (iron, phosphates and minor elements such as copper, zinc and manganese) cannot be released and the shrub will be deficient in these elements and eventually prove a failure. Thus one should lime only when it is known that a plant is particular larly fond of lime and can "take" any amount of it, or when there is proof that the soil lacks lime. Lavender makes a lovely little hedge in the garden but has an annoying habit of dying out. A good application of lime will end this seemingly mysterious habit.

There are various methods of making the soil more acid, in order to benefit acid-loving plants. An ideal good garden soil is always very slightly acid, the pH being slightly above 6. Many shrubs prefer a soil that is very acid, with a pH as low as 4, and should be grown together in a separate portion of the garden or can be treated individually.

One of the quickest methods is the use of aluminium sulphate, which is a powder that can be obtained from wholesale suppliers of chemicals. This must be used sparingly but in sufficient quantity to maintain the required degree of acidity. On the average, used sparingly but in sufficient quantity to maintain the required degree of acidity. On the average, this should be used on ordinary garden soils at the rate of handfuls to the square yard. Where soils are strongly alkaline, a large quantity is required. Sprinkle this powder around the base of the shrub and water it in. wait for several weeks and repeat the procedure. Even if this is done only a couple of months before the flowering season, the results of the readjustment of the soil can often be seen, and in the case of the once barren Azalea, which likes an acid soil, a sheet of bloom will appear once more in the spring.

Another successful chemical is commercial tannic acid which can be used in much the same way. It has the added advantage of being organic material. It is made chiefly from the bark of Wattle trees, is manufactured in Natal and can be bought quite cheaply in blocks. A readily available from of tannic acid, which should appeal to all gardeners, is present in used tea-leaves. After the gardener has enjoyed his cup of tea, he should pour the contents of the pot at the base of his acid-loving shrubs. In order to save up the precious tea-leaves without always running out into the garden, a stone jar should be kept in the kitchen, into which all the dregs should be thrown. As this is filled, the gardener can transfer it to the shrubs. The tea-leaves dry-loving shrubs such as Azaleas, Camellias, Gardenias, Magnolias and *Leptospermum.* A friend of mine, who gave this treatment to his purple Magnolia, was amazed at the way the hitherto small, stunted shrub grew long vigorous stems with large, healthy green leaves in a single season. He thereupon coined a phrase, which amusingly sums up the whole situation, "It's always tea-time for Magnolias."

Other mulches of organic materials which contain acid may be used around the base of acid-loving shrubs. These include certain leaves, particularly those of Oak and the Sumac trees, as well as Pine-neeles. Other suitable materials for acid mulches are the rotted bark of trees such as Chestnuts, Oakes, Gums, Pines and Wattles; well-rotted sawdust or ground acorns. All these mulches should be replaced or added to from time to time, as the acid is leached out by watering. Some acid-loving shrubs such as Rhododendrons, need a thick, permanent mulch of leaves around the base in order to roots from drying out. Most acid-loving shrubs like a light, porous soil, and, as a general rule, should be planted with masses of compost.

It is interesting to note that the colours of Hydrangeas can be changed by readjusting the pH of the soil. Pink Hydrangeas like a very slightly acid soil (pH 6) while blue Hydrangeas like a strongly acid soil (pH 4.5). the addition of lime will turn them pink and the addition of aluminium sulphate will turn them blue. In both cases water the root with a weak solution of the powder (1oz. to 1 gallon) about once a month. Incidentally, eosin makes them very dark red.

All lawns love lime which is frequently sprinkled over them. A difficult arises when acid-loving shrubs are planted in the lawn. The gardener must not do well, as the rain washes the lime from one part of the soil to the other. In the same way, acid-loving shrubs should not be planted up the bed might cause deterioration of the shrub.

All these methods of making the soil more acid or more alkaline should be repeated at least once or twice a year, as many things, such as rainwater and earthworms, tend to alter the soil reaction and the soil loses its acidity or alkalinity in time.

Chapter 5

Propagation and Planning

In South almond tree that has taken nine years to grow to a height of 12 feet in England, will reach that height in South Africa in about four years. For the amateur gardener and the possessor of a new garden, this fact has a very definite advantage in that it is possible to build up a gardener that looks quite well established in a third of the time that it would take in Europe.

The gardener can do many things to hasten growth and that well-established look by careful attention to watering and general care as well as by planting sizeable shrubs and trees from nurseries.

Methods of Raising Shrubs and Trees

The idea of idea *growing a shrub or tree from seed* very laborious to the home gardener, but in fact, it is very often easy and quick. Some trees do much better when they are grown from seed and planted out when quite small. This is true of *Bauhinia variegate* which grows a long tap root very rapidly and is best planted out while only three inches high and easy to handle. It very often flowers in the third year of planting, attains a height and spread of eight feet in four years and has a much more natural and compact shape if grown from seed than if bought in a tin, where it is usually grown with a long stem.

On the other hand it is really too much for the gardener to expect to grow Azaleas, which are particularly difficult, or any other slow growing shrub from seed, as it takes a quite a low figure. The average shrub costs no more than a tray of annual plants, and when one considers the everlasting value of the former it is surprising that the average garden does not have more shrubs in it.

Our indigenous South Africa shrubs and trees grow very easily from seed and in fact can be grown almost without exception from seed. Growing them from seed enables them to acclimatize themselves in different parts of the country away from their natural home. The Silver tree, which grows on Table Mountain, can be grown vey easily from seed and adjusts itself to the cold winter of the Transvaal, whereas it seldom survives transplanting. It will reach a size of six feet in about three years, particularly if it is pampered by lots of water during winter (to simulate the winter rainfall of the Cape) and has some protection from frost in the way of a sheltering wall or rock, in the early stages of growth.

The National Botanic Gardens at Kirstenbosch supply seed of many indigenous shrubs, tree and plants of all descriptions. These seeds are unobtainable from ordinary seed shops and are supplied only to membership is very inexpensive, and in return for subscriptions paid supplied only to members. Membership is very inexpensive, and in return for subscriptions paid, packets of seed, which can be chosen from a seed list issued each year, are supplied to members annually. Every garden lover should belong to Kirstenbosch, for apart from his personal gains, he will be helping to maintain the gardens, which depend to a large extent on the support of the public. The botanists at Kirstenbosch are helping to preserve our natural flora which gives pleasure to gardenrs all over the world. Many treasures are available to us through their efforts and the gardens at Kirstenbosch represent a beautiful example of how our natural heritage is being nartured, so that the enemies of the plants, in the shape of forest fires and vandalism can be combated.

Some nurseries supply South Africa shrubs and there are a few in particular that devote all their efforts to supplying indigenous or native bulbs and plants as well as seeds, so that the busy gardener need not bother to plant seeds at all.

A great number of shrubs and trees can be grown from seed without much trouble, however, and in much the same way as ordinary annuals. Prepare tins in the same way as they are prepared for flower seeds, with small stones for drainage at the bottom and filled with a mixture of good soil and compost. The addition of vermiculite mixed with the soil aids water retention and makes the germination of seeds almost always successful. Large seeds should be planted in individual tins as this makes them much easier to handle for transplanting.

Very large, hard-skinned seeds can be forced to germinate mote quickly in a number of ways. They can be soacked in water for several days or until their skins split and then planted out, although there is a danger here that they might rot; some, such as the ACACIA seeds, need to be softened in boiling water; they can also be scratched slightly with a razor blade on the smooth side, but one must be very careful not to damage the scar which marks the point where the seedling emerges.

The golden rule of covering any seed with a layer of soil not thicker than its own diameter, applies to the seeds of trees or shrubs. The tins should be covered with a piece of hessian which is removed only when watering, and removed completely when the seedling has emerged.

One disadvantage of growing shrubs and trees from seed is that the improved varieties often revert back to the original parent and the new characteristics are often lost. Also it is not always likely that the flowers will be the same colour as those of the parent plant, so that if one wants to obtain the identical plant, the best way to do is to take cuttings.

Cuttings

These are often easy to take. Success varies with the individual species and it is always interesting to experiment for oneself depending on the patience of the grower. Some trees, such as the WILLOW, strike so easily from cutting that if their twigs are used to make a "fence" to keep the dogs off a bed in the garden, they will often produce leaves and begin to grow. The time to take cutting is in spring or autumn.

A cutting can be cut from a fairly stalh of a shrub nea the tip. A piece of roughly nine inches is a good length may vary considerably. The main requirement is that it should be cut cleanly at a point immediately below the junction of a leaf with the stem. Another way of taking a cutting, is to break off a short side branch in such a way that the stem. Another way of taking a cutting, is to break off a short side branch in such a way that a heel or piece of the main stem is left on it. Cuttings can also be made of very soft young wood at the growing tip, in which case the cut should also be made just below the junction of a leaf and stem.

All leaves except the top ones should be pulled off and two-thirds of the cutting should be inserted into a in tin containing damp river sand. This should be kept damp and preferably in the shade. When the leaves show signs of growing or alternatively the cutting has been pulled out and seen to have grown four to eight weeks. Sometimes, as in the case of POINSETTIA, the cuttings, may be planted directly into the position where they are to grow and not disturbed any further. Other cuttings, such as those of ROSEMARY, can be handled as above.

Layers are formed when a branch of a shrub is bent over and kept in contact with ground, by means of either a peg or stones, and which will grow roots at that point. When it has grown roots the branch can be cut away from the parent plant and will grow the ground, as is the case with *Cotoneaster horizontalis.* This does require attention, however, and is not as quick or easy as taking a cutting.

Grafting and Budding are two methods of propagation best left to the nurseryman or the really enthusiastic gardener who wishes to make a study of this art. It is complicated, and needs a great deal of attention, knowledge and experience. *Propagation by division* is an easy method of acquiring a new stalks at the ground, in the autumn, winter or spring, in the same way as many perennials are increased by division. This method is usually completely successful.

Size to Plant Out

Tree roots grow rapidly so that trees should be planted out as young as possible. If you have grown your own tree or shrub from seed, it follows that you will transplant it into the garden when it is much young than any tree that you may buy.

When roots grow rapidly so that trees should be planted out as young as possible. If you have grown your own tree or shrub from seed, it follows that you will transplant it into the garden when it is much younger than any tree that you may buy.

When buying shrubs which are established in tins, they may be planted at any size as their roots are confined to the tin. It is always best not to plant trees that are too big as their roots may be pot-bound and badly tangled. It usually takes a large tree at least two seasons to establish itself and begin to fill out its foliage, so that there is not really much gain in time. Some trees, such as *Melia azedarach* (SYRINGA) grow more rapidly if planted small. A large one is apt to remain static in growth for many years, while a younger one will outstrip it and from a better shape.

The only time that it is a definite advantage to buy large specimens in tins is when they are very slow growing, and one can save a number of years, as in the case of Magnolias. But here again the shrub must not be too large in proportion to its roots.

Plant and Transplant Time

There are two definite sets of rules which apply to the planting out or transplanting of shrubs and trees. One rule applies to *evergreen trees,* which do not lose their leaves in winter, and another rule to *deciduous trees,* which lose their leaves during the winter months.

Neither of these rules applies to trees and shrubs which are bought established in tins from nurseries, for these may be planted out at any time of the year without danger of loss. Early spiring is the best time to plant any shrub, for that is the time when all growth begins and the newly planted shrub will grow and establish itself well before the following winter. Spring is the best time to plant all tender shrubs, when all danger of cold and frost is over, and they may have a whole season in which to establish themselves before the cold weather comes again.

The rules for planting out evergreens or deciduous trees apply to trees and shrubs which are being moved from the open ground, that is, when they are not in tins.

Transplanting Deciduous Trees

Many nurseries supply *deciduous tree* from the open ground. This is only at one time of the year, in June and July when the sap is at its lowest and the trees are leafless and dormant. It is cheaper to buy trees from the open ground as the nurseries are saved the expense trees from the open ground when people are careless about one simple requirement. The roots must not be allowed to dry out even for a half-hour, nor must the wind the air be allowed to get at them, or they may never recover. Do not buy a tree from the open the ground, therefore, unless the hole has been prepared and is waiting for the tree, or when you will not have time to plant it on arrival. Also see that the roots are covered with a wt sack until you are completely ready to plant. Immediately on planting, water copiously.

When transplanting deciduous trees from one part of the garden to the other, the same procedure should be followed. Before removing the trees, tie a handkerchief to mark a branch of the tree which faces north, and be sure to plant the tree in its new position with the same branch facing north. This will help to keep constant the position of the tree in relation to the sun. in transplanting, extra care is needed to dig out the tree. If the ground is very hard, water it well the day before so that it will be softened. Then dig a narrow trench around the base of the tree at a distance from the trunk, varying from 18 inches to three according to the size of the tree. In this way it is possible to see how far the roots of the tree have spread. If they are very large, the circle should be made bigger. One will have tio sever some roots and it is best to cut them off cleanly with a sharp cutter. When the trench is finished the tree will remain standing with a ring of earth around it. One should now try to dig undernearth this earth in order to lift the whole "ball" of earth together with the tree without disturbing it. Some soil will naturally fall away, but provided that one keeps the part immediately around the centre of the root intact, there is no danger of loss. If the roots of the tree are deep, the trench will have to be deepended, but it is nearly always necessary to sever the main roots so that the tree can be handled easily, and this can usually be done with safety.

The nurseries usually cut back the branches of the tree to balance the cutting back of the roots, and this serves the double purpose of allowing root growth to compete with leaf growth in the spring and to allow for easy transport and storage. In one's own garden, however, this need not be done, as it frequently spoils the shape. Only very small twiggy growths need be removed, unless the tree is really very big, in which case it can be cut back more severely.

Transplanting Evergreens

Evergreen trees are never supplied by nurserymen from the open ground as they would never survive. If evergreens are to be transplanted from one part of the garden to the other, this should be done only in the spring and during rainy weather.

After transplanting, evergreens require even more water than deciduous trees as the fact that the leaves are always on the tree makes them lose water more rapidly. It has been proved that the leaves pull up water from the roots like a magnet, and that is not pumped growth the leaves draw up as much water as they need, but the transplanted root system is not able to continue this flow uninterruptedly, for it must first establish itself. In the leaves may wither and die, and not being there to draw up the sap, the sap may die down too. Unless the plant is watered copiously, it may die altogether.

It is important, therefore, to slow up evaporation from the leaves so that thay do not demand a great deal of water the root system, at least for a while until the shrub has established itself. The moisture in the air during the rainy weather, as well as the falling rain, will slow up evaporation. In addition, the leaves can be sprayed with water trickling from the hosepipe, for 24 hours at a stretch if necessary until one can see an obvious sign that the shrub has "taken." This may be seen by the growth of a new leaf, but in the case of evergreens, one must wait until a leaf grows before you cease your vigilance.

Frequently the leaves of evergreen will wither or die in a day or two a there has not been enough food supply, but one must continue to water copiously until the shrub has taken. Do not pull out a transplanted evergreen when it looks as if it has died. Care for it for several months, or even a complete season, and eventually you may encourage the sap to rise and it may send out a new strong shoot from the base. There is nothing like a number of days of rain to help an evergreen to re-establish itself in a new environment.

When transplanting evergreens, as with deciduous trees, the same system of digging around the trunk should be employed. Here, however, it is so important to retain the ball of earth around the roots, that this should be wrapped with hessian which is preferably dampened, and tied securely with string before digging undernearth the tree. As the root is severed at the bottom, and the tree is tipped over to one side, more hessian should be wrapped around the base in order to prevent the soil from falling away. The tree is now "balled" and can be planted with the hessian around it. The hessian will rot in time and the tree roots will grow throough it, but this does help to prevent any dislodging of the delicate root hairs which are so necessary for the absorption of water through the roots. With evergreens, it is all a question of how quickly the tree can establish its normal routine of water absorption.

Cutting back of evergreens is usually recommended so that there will be fewer leaves to supply with food and water, and there will, therefore, be less of a strain on the root system. There is a danger in cutting back evergreens indiscriminately, as many evergreens, such as MAGNOLIAS, thoroughly dislike pruning and one can do more harm by cutting back such a shrub than not. Stripping of most of the leaves, would be better idea in such cases.

Nothing gives the gardener a greater thrill than to transplant a tree or shrub successfully, but one should be prepared for the risks involved. As trees become older and larger, it becomes increasingly difficult to transplant them. The size at which one can transplant varies with each tree. A EUCALYPTUS should not be transplanted when it has grown large than three feet, while an OAK tree can be transplanted up to 15 feet or more. Generally speaking, one can transplant deciduous trees almost up to any size, while evergreens are best transplanted when small. Some trees are quite easy to handle. So one can see that there is risk involved in transplanting, which should not be done unless it is absolutely necessary, for even the most expertly transplanted tree will suffer a setback and slow down in growth for a while until it is completely established. It is always safer to transplant established shrubs from tins as this ensures no loss.

How to Plant

The ground should always be well prepared before planting.

Preparing the Ground

There is a controversy about digging holes for trees and shrubs as some say that this disturbs the subsoil. Where the soil is known to be rich and deep, then one can dig small holes, but if the ground so that the tree can thrive for the first few years of its life until its root system grows beyond the limits of the hole prepared for it and can carry on growing from there. It is surprising what small roots some trees do have. I transplanted an eight-years-old oak, and found the root span to be 150 cm and the depth 60 cm.

The hole should be prepared with compost which is always excellent. Manure can also be used at the bottom of the hole. In the case of fast growing trees, this may foolish according to some, but at least it carries the young tree through the first few years and stimulates faster growth.

The size of the hole varies with the gardener's energy. The site for this particular OAK tree was rockey and poor, so we dug a hole 2.4 m^2 and 1.8 m deep and removed all the rocks. Then we filled up with sub-soil, manure and good top soil mixed compost. After planting the tree we put the hosepipe on it for two days, night and day, until the ground was saturated. Continue water twice a week for days, night and day, until the tree put on its first leaves in the spring and for 30 days afterwards. Later we reduced the time of watering, merely filling the large "basin" made round the tree twice a week. This may sound extreme, but the oak thrived and bore acorn where before, neglected and never watered, it had never done so. This treatment shows the extreme to which the gardener will go to pamper his treasures.

The average hole should be at least two to three feet across and the same depth. Drainage should be provided at the bottom in the form of a layer of small several inches thick. There are some who say that this is unnecessary as the water cannot drain further. It is true that one could make a perfectly drained spot by constructing a bank, several feet high, built on a foundation of rubbish and stones, but this is not always possible. For practical purposes, we should ty and provide a certain amount of drainage, which, even if it is useful only for the first few years of the shrub's life have helped towards its establishment.

The bottom half of the hole should be filled with soil and manure mixed. Use the subsoil if it is not too poor and gravelly, otherwise substitute with ordinary garden soil. the manure will enrich the bottom soil and stimulate the shrub when its roots reach it in the following seasons, the top half of the hole should consist of good garden soil mixed generously with compost.

Planting

First put down a five- or six –inch layer of the mixture of compost and soul on top of the manured soil, so that the shrub roots will not come in contact with the manure for some time, and then pile the centre of the soil into a small mound. Place the shrub or tree-hairs, and these must be in close contact with the earth, or they will shrivel in a vacuum of air. Then begin to fill up the hole with the remaining soil and compost, stopping half-way to tramp the soil well down all around and up to the base of the stem. The tree will now be firmly planted in the ground and it will not be possible to dislodge its position its position easily. Finish off with the soil level at the top.

Do not plant the shrub deeper than it was planted before. The mark on the stem where the soil reached before is quite easily seen, for the bark is a different colour. Trees and shrubs planted too deeply might die months or even years after planting.

See that the soil level of the hole is slightly below that of the surrounding soil or lawn. This forms a "basin" in which the water can collect and aids watering.

Immediately after planting, without losing any time, the shrub must be thoroughly soaked with water. The equivalent of two buckets of water must be given, and in the case of a transplanted tree, the hosepipe should be left to trickle slowly into the hole for several hours.

This applies to trees planted out from the open ground or transplanted. When shrubs are bought from the nursery already established in tins, the procedure is slightly different. Prepare the hole in exactly the same way as before, with the manured soil at the bottom half of the hole. Meanwhile soak the tin in water so that it is thoroughly damp. This is most important as no amount of watering afterwards will penetrate the solid block of soil and really soak it. This also prevents tearing the delicate roots away from the sides of the tin. Then cute away the tin with a sharp pair of tin snips or a tin opener. Cut down all four corners of the tin, so that the sides can be opened flat, being careful not to damage the roots of the plant. Some thoughtful nurserymen supply tins that can be unhooked and opened without a struggle.

Then lift the complete "ball" of earth gently and place it on top of the layer of soil and compost, trying not to let any of it crumble off. Fill up all rounds with the remaining soil and compost as before tramping it down firmly in the same way. There is no need to worry about the level of planting, as the level of the soil in the tin should be the correct level. Let the hosepipe trickle into the hole as before, until the ground is thoroughly saturated.

There is practically no risk of losing a shrub planted out in this way as the root system is not disturbed. It is only when the roots are roughly handled and not well watered that a shrub is lost. Some shrubs such as Leptospermum, the Australian tea-treee, so dislike their roots to be handled, that many people merely cut off the bottom of the tin and plant the shrub with the sides of the tin encasing its roots. In time the tin will rot and the roots will grow through it, but if the few simple instructions above are carried out, there need be no risk of loss.

Staking

Any shrub ar small tree that has a slender stem is planted, for it might damage the roots if driven into the ground at a later date. Place the stak alongside the tree before the roots are covered with soil. Then fill in the soil firmly around both the tree and the stake. In this way the stake will be as firmly planted in the earth as the tree and will not bend in the wind.

Do not tie the stake closely to the stem of the young tree, for as it grows, the twine will cut into the bark and cut off the supply of food to the leaves, so that the may die eventually. More suddenly, the tree will snap off in a strong wind, the stem being literally sawn off by the twine. Wrap a piece of hessian around the stem and tie a piece of twin around it. Then tie the other end of the twine around the stake, keeping the stem erect. All too often people see that the stake and not the stem of the tree, is erect. One should remove the hessian every six months and re tie it in a different spot. This enables the trunk to grow evenly and prevents damage to the bark which may leave an entry for disease. As soon as the trunk thickens and the tree is sturdy enough to stand by itself, remove the stake altogether.

Two stakes, at a small distance apart on the one side of the tree, are often necessary when the tree is tall or top-heavy. Take particular notice of the prevailing winds and support the tree so that the wind cannot bend it over, by placing the stakes on the same side as the direction from which the wind blows. Many people allow their trees to grow without forming a "standard" in their natural bushy from, these tree will seldom require staking.

Chapter 6

Principles of Landscape Designs

Landscaping is an art and horticultural-based science; the landscape architect/designer should apply the principles of planting design and make judicious use of landscape elements for an artistic composition.

Landscape gardening is the application of garden forms, methods and materials to the improvement of the landscape and the landscape in this connection is any area, large or small, on which it is possible or desirable to develop a view or a design. The planning of a garden is an art. A garden architect should learn enough of geology, geography, garden history, styles of gardening, and above all should have a profound knowledge about plants.

Some of the terminologies used in landscaping are as follows.

Landscape

"A landscape is as any area on which it is possible to mould a view or a design".

Landscape Gardening

Landscape gardening is an application of garden forms, methods and materials with a view to improve the landscape. The art of designing is known as 'landscape architecture,' earlier known as 'Landscape gardening' is also well known.

Gardening

Following points should be considered before implementing gardening.

1. Do not to imitate another garden which has secured a prize in a competition.
2. One has to develop one's own design giving due consideration to the local conditions.
3. Do not plant many more specimens than a garden can accommodate causing overcrowding.
4. In a landscape garden any difference in levels has to be taken advantage of, but in a perfectly flat land it will be costly to create artificial undulations.
5. In each garden there should be at least one feature or if there be a second these two should harmonize with each other.
6. Before planning a design one must be sure for what purpose the garden is – utility or beauty or both.

Principles of Gardening

- In theory, everyone would like to have a perfect plot of land, but in actual practice the plot available for gardening, in three out of five cases, either will not be in a good site or the shape and size will not be ideal. A good designer is one who will make best use of such a site. As has already been stated, land with natural undulations should never be leveled, but rather the differences in levels should be utilized with advantage. Fencing, should be such that it looks natural as far as practicable and it should not obstruct any natural view. For example, if there is natural forest scenery or a hillock just outside the boundary, it should be incorporated in the garden design in a thoughtful manner so that it appears to be a part of the garden.
- This is an imaginary line in any garden around which the garden is created striking a balance. In a formal garden, the central line is the axis. At the end of an axis, generally there will be a focal point, although other architectural features such as bird-bath or sundial can also be erected at about the midpoint.
- In every garden there is a centre of attraction which is generally an architectural feature focused as a point of interest such as statue, fountain, rockery *etc.* A focal point is one of the elements of good landscape design.
- The use of one general form of plant material in large numbers in one place is done to have mass effect. To see that such mass arrangements do not become monotonous, the sizes of masses should be varied.
- Unity in a garden is very important as when this is achieved it will improve the artistic look of the garden. Unity has to be achieved from various angles.

First, the unity of style, feeling, and function between the house and the garden has to be achieved. Secondly, the different components of the gardens should merge harmoniously with each other. The aim is to give the visitor an overall impression of the garden rather than blowing up some special features. The last point, which is also very important, is to achieve some harmony between the landscape outside and the garden. A garden laid out in complete defiance of the local conditions may look exotic, but is not a successful garden. As for example, cacti planted in a seashore garden is completely out of place as these are inhabitants of dry localities.

To achieve a unity between the house and the garden it is a common practice to train creepers on the front porch which cover the rudeness of the masonry work and also bring the house closer to nature. For the same reasons, foundation plantings are also done. A foundation planting broadly means the planting of bushy plants near the foundation of the house.

- ☆ The garden should appear larger than its actual size. One way of achieving this is to keep vast open spaces, preferably under lawn and restrict the plantings in the periphery, normally avoiding any planting in the centre. But if any planting has to be done in the centre the choice should be a tree which branches at a higher level on the trunk (or the lower branches are removed), and not a bushy shrub. Such planting will not abstract the view or make the garden appear smaller than its size. Another suggestion to create the illusion of more space in a large public garden is to alternate large lawns followed by a group of trees. A large open space planted haphazardly all over with trees looks smaller than its size. **The techniques of creating an illusion of more** space are also referred to as 'Forced Perspective'.
- ☆ In a landscape garden, there should not be any hard and fast divisional lines. But there is the necessity of dividing or rather screening a compost pit or a Mali's quarter or a vegetable garden from the rest of the garden. In fact areas under lawn, gravel, stone or cement path, and shrubbery border have their natural divisional lines from its immediate neighbour though these are not discreet. This is what is exactly needed. The divisional lines should be artistic with gentle curves and these should also be useful. Above all these lines should harmonize with one another.
- ☆ Proportion in a garden may be defined as a definite relationship between masses. For example, a rectangle having a ratio of 5:8 is considered to be of pleasing proportion. As this ratio comes down the form looks neither a square nor a rectangle and the design becomes undesirable.

  There is no set rule as regards scale or proportion in a garden. But a simple rule is that a design should look pleasant. It is better to have an *ad-hoc* design first and then try it out on the actual spot. If the design looks appealing as well as pleasing, it is implemented. When a shrubbery border has to be planted the outer design is marked by arranging a rubber hose or thick wet rope in different designs on the spot and the one, which looks best, is adopted. Then sticks of different heights, representing the various shrubs, are planted in various positions and by the method of permutation and combination the most proportionate looking arrangement is adopted.

The common practice of laying out a small rockery at the base of a large tree with small rockery at the base of a large tree with small thorny specimens looks not only ugly but is also out of scale and proportion under the large canopy of the tree. A tiny pool in the midst of a large lawn also looks disproportionate.

☆ The surface character of a garden unit is referred to as texture. The texture of the ground, the leaves of a tree or shrub will all determine the overall effect of the garden. The texture of rugged looking ground can be improved to an appreciable extent by laying meticulously chosen small pebbles from the riverbeds, if establishing a lawn is out of the question.

A *Gulmohar* (*Delonix rezia*) is a fine textured tree when in full leaf, whereas African tulip tree (*Spathodea companulata*) is a coarse textured tree. The placement of all these various textures with harmony and contrast has to be achieved to get the ultimate desirable effect.

☆ In a garden the time factor is very important. There are three different categories of time in a garden.

(*i*) The daily time, which provides different quantities and qualities of light during the course of the day. As the morning sun is vital for all flowers, the designer has to take this into account while planning. In most parts of India the garden design should be planned in such a way that in the afternoon it is possible to sit in a shaded place from where the best part of the garden should be visible.

(*ii*) The seasonal changes in the year. A good planner must roughly take into account the seasonal movement of the sun and where the shade and light are likely to fall during the different parts of the season.

(*iii*) The fact as to what shape and proportion the shrubs and trees will attain in the years to come. Often we can see sickly and lanky shrubs growing near the trunk of a large tree, because of lack of light and possibly nutrients also. The shrubs were planted when the tree was a sapling, without visualizing what would happen to them when the tree attained its full size. The right type of tree should be planted at the proper place so that shade is obtained during the hot days, at the appropriate time.

☆ A tendency on the part of an amateur Gardner is to create a riot of colours by indiscriminately planting flowering annuals of all shades. This practice is not desirable. Moreover, such riot of colours has only temporary effect. In a landscape garden, the permanent backdrop is the green tones of the various trees and shrubs. It is possible to lay out a garden with subtle tone of entirely white or yellow flowers, but at the same time making it charming also. Another important point is that it is better to have masses of a single colour against a mixture of colours. A bud of roses containing only a single colour of say red, yellow, or pink has a much softer tone and beauty than a bed containing a mixture of colours.

☆ In a temperate country, the garden changes colour very sharply and contrastingly from one season to the other thus symbolizing mobility or movement. As for example, many trees in the temperate regions attire themselves with wonderful hues due to the changes in their leaf colour in the autumn.

In most parts of Tropical India, though these contrasting changes cannot be achieved, it is possible to bring in some subtle changes. For example, to create some symbol of movement trees such as Bengal or Indian Almond (*Terminalia catappa*) which changes its leaf colour into striking red twice annually before falling or Pride of India which also changes the colour of the leaves to coppery shade in the autumn before shedding, or Indian butter tree and Pipal, the new foliage of these appearing as coppery red in the spring, should be planted in some parts of the garden. This, in addition, improves the landscape.

The movement and cluttering of birds also brings life and mobility to the garden, though sometimes some birds may become a menace. Large trees and bird-baths attract birds. For the smaller birds, the safety of shrubberies is needed to protect them from large predator birds.

Some plants, bearing berries, such as *Ficus infectoria* and *Syzygium cumini,* can also be planted in some remote corners though they may not look very ornamental. Flowering trees such as silk cotton or *Erythrina* also attract birds when in bloom.

The seasonal flowers will bring in the motion and movement of colourful butterflies. Fountains or even a lawn sprinkler and streams in a garden also serve the objective of movement. The lily pools should be filled with coloured fish, the movement of which will be an added attraction. The frogs will also come and inhabit these pools uninvite4d and in the process bring in more movement.

☆ One has to decide about the style to be adopted for one's garden. Broadly speaking, every garden lover has to invent his own style of gardening commensurate with his budget, taste and the nature of the site. But a one can develop ones own design only when one studies carefully all the great garden styles of the world and grasps the underlying principles in them. There is no doubt that persons not having enough specialized knowledge will commit mistakes; nevertheless, one should not get deterred by this fact.

Chapter 7

Garden Elements, Designs

Landscape architects have several elements that are important in the making of a garden or outdoor space. Ultimately, it is the details that make a space successful. The combination of those materials and how the materials work together is also important. The grouping of these elements with each other is as vital as how these elements agree with the principles of design such as unity, variety, balance, centre of interest or focal point, rhythm, colour, texture, scale, proportion and their relationships. Also light, sound, smell and texture are important things to keep in mind. A garden must be a source of stimulation of the senses and therefore, elements which interact with the senses must be used. Food can also be seen as an element and in a park or plaza, without food, would not be as enjoyable. There are many more elements that may be used in landscape architecture. However, the mentioned above are the most common and are used for Planting; Paving – Walks, patios, terraces, decks, plazas, courts, playing surfaces; Shelters- Overheads, trellises, canopies and other such structures; Screens and fences; Retaining walls; Elevation changes-steps, ramps and embankments'; Bridges; Lighting; Furniture-Benches, chairs, tables, waste containers; Information – Kiosks, signage, graphics; Art-Sculptures, murals, fountains, banners, mosaics *etc.* and Water-Fountains, pools, drinking water.

Very important elements in landscaping are:

☆ **Major elements**: plants and water

- **Minor elements**: Stones, bricks, tiles, tar, metal, grass, plastic, wood, sculpture *etc.*
- **Other elements**: Light, sound, smell, touch, food *etc.*

Major Elements

1. Plants

The designer should first decide about the garden design before deciding which plants to be used. Plants can be used for functional and aesthetic reasons and their physical appearance should be kept in mind. Plants can be used for various reasons. They help to control solar radiation, act as windbreak, control soil erosion, control air, noise, dust pollution *etc.*, as they act as barriers and trap the prevailing noise, dust and so on. Plants are also used for architectural aspect. They create space and define areas. They screen, buffer and provide privacy. They have the biggest ability to beautify the surrounding to provide a healthy, green view to the eyes, they provide support to a number of animals and birds and create a lively garden.

Plant materials have many sensory qualities. We can see their various forms, textures, and colours. We can feel their textures, we can smell their fragrances. We can even taste their foliage, blooms, and fruit. In order to create a pleasing landscape design, we must co-ordinate the functional uses of plants with our sensory perceptions. The plants are classified for different purpose as discussed

1. Aesthetic Purpose

(a) Avenue planting- flower parade
(b) Ground planting
(c) Shrubbery, rockery, topiary, hedges, edges
(d) Potted plant, flower beds, boarders
(e) Ground cover
(f) Water garden

2. Functional Purpose

(a) Control pollution
(b) Reduces noise
(c) Control soil erosion
(d) Wind break
(e) Deciduous plants can utilize to increase temperature during winter

Criteria for Selection of Plants

Some of the important morphological character should be considered while selecting the plants;

1. Height of the plant
2. Types of branches- upright, drooping, horizontal

3. Spread and width of the plant
4. Form of the plat
5. Type of plant- evergreen, deciduous
6. Colour of the plant
7. Texture of the plant- smooth, rough
8. Flowering time of the plant

2. Water

water has the ability to change form, at low temperature water freezes, evaporates at high temperature and liquefies at moderate temperature:

Aesthetic Use

- ☆ Waterfalls- cascade type, fountains, streams, lakes, ponds, Nappe, Chadar, chute.
- ☆ Water is used for creating reflection during night time along with lighting.
- ☆ The use of water helps in reducing the temperature in the microclimate.
- ☆ Sound of water makes a person feel comfortable.
- ☆ Water may mask the over power unwanted sounds

Functional Use

Water will nourish the plant, increases growth and development

Minor Elements

1. Stones

- ☆ For creating rockery, statues or sculptures, to imitate natural water falls, garden benches, path/walks
- ☆ Stone radiates heat and will have to be used carefully

2. Bricks

- ☆ For creating garden walls, ponds
- ☆ As paving material
- ☆ For constructing plant boxes

3. Wood

- ☆ Wood adds colour and texture to the garden
- ☆ Used for creating paths, steps, garden bridges, ornamental picket fence, country fences, arches, pergolas
- ☆ Wood should be coated with paints/preservatives to prevent decay

4. Metal

- For creating artistic features like garden bridges, arches, pergolas, Arbour, fence, light stands, metal gardens
- Used as a base material for plants to grow on, when used for topiary
- Metals should be treated with anti corrosive materials before using in the out doors

5. Sculptures

- Artistic material adds beauty to the garden with the use of stones, granites, sandstone, marbles, metals
- Sculptures includes birds, human being, animals *etc.*
- It can be kept in front, middle part, and in running streams of the garden

6. Glass

It includes mist chamber, green house, conservatory, terrariums and illumination purpose

7. Concrete

Used for creating drives, paths, walks, ground cover

8. Tar/Asphalt

Creating drives

9. Plastic

Drippers, sprinklers, pots, waste bin

Other Elements

1. Lighting

Illumination, focusing the focal points, illuminating water

2. Sound

Waterfalls, running streams, musical fountain, and wind chimes

3. Smell

Planting of aromatic plants in different parts of the garden, trees, aromatic plants, annual beds can be used.

4. Touch

Texture of materials like plant surface, sculptures, paving, garden benches.

5. Food

Created at outside boundary of the garden

Basic Pattern in Garden Design

1. Circular Pattern

Series of circles can utilize to create circular. It is used in formal and informal gardens

2. Diagonal Pattern

Draws a grid line at 45° to the boundary. It is also used in formal and informal gardens

3. Rectangular Pattern

It is utilized in formal garden in a symmetrical manner

Stepts in Garden Design

- **Identification of site:** Identify the site for two purposes:
  1. Public garden: give importance for likings of the public
  2. Private garden: Give importance for owners comfort
- **Analysis:** Need to study two factors
  1. Physical factor- climate, weather, soil type, existing vegetation, existing manholes, roads, path
  2. Social factors
- **Measuring up**: Draw rough sketch of the area like existing features, length and width of all features
- **Drawing to the scale:** based on sheet available for small garden 1: 50 and for big garden 1: 100
- **Evolving a pattern:** Fence, lawn, flower beds, hedge, edge, border, water falls, rock garden, pond, shrubbery, island beds, carpet beds, standards *etc.*
- **Turning pattern in to reality:** Mark the area using pegs and bars and plant the permanent features on marked ground
- Xeriscaping: It is landscaping and gardening that reduces or eliminates the need for supplemental water from irrigation. This is a technique use to practice water conservation in creative landscape, this can be practiced in areas where scarcity of water

Advantages

- Lowered consumption of water
- Makes more water available for other domestic and community uses and the environment.
- Reduce Maintenance: Aside from occasional weeding and mulching Xeriscaping requires far less time and effort to maintain.

- Xeriscape plants in appropriate planting design and soil grading and mulching, takes full advantage of rainfall retention.
- Less cost to maintain: Xeriscaping requires less fertilizers and equipment, particularly due to the reduced lawn areas.
- Reduced waste and pollution

Chapter 8

Propagation of Ornamental Plants

The animates reproduce by producing off-spring or by multiplying themselves. In nature plants propagate themselves by seeds and vegetative parts. The gardener has to learn the different methods of propagation to replace the old or the diseased stocks and to meet the increasing demand of a growing garden. Plants are propagated either sexual or asexual means. Some kinds of plants are propagated by both the methods.

Methods of Propagation

There are different methods of plant propagation, which can be classified under two heads: (A) Sexual Propagation (B) Asexual or vegetative propagation.

(A) Sexual Propagation

Plants are propagated sexually by seeds and spores. Likewise in ferns. But, when this falls on a moist surface it produces small plant bodies (prothallia), which develops the sex organs (archegonia and antheridia) and these in due course develop sex elements (gametes), which fuse and resulting body develops into the fern plant.

It is generally observed that plants raised from seeds are more vigorous in growth than those raised by vegetative methods. A seedlings may not be an exact replica of the parents as a result of natural cross-fertilization or segregation of characters, whereas plants raised by vegetative means resemble the mother plant in all plant characters unless the plant part used for propagation turns out to be a natural 'sort'. Propagation by seed is necessary to obtain new plants or hybrids.

One disadvantage of propagation from seeds is that the seedling may take years to produce flowers. For example, an orchid seedling may take 5-8 years to produce flowers. But a plant raised by vegetative propagation from another mature plant flowers within a season or between 1 and 2 years.

Controlling Germination of Seeds

It is difficult or rather impossible to get 100 per cent germination, even when the seeds are sown in a perfect condition, for a variety of reasons. The factors which control germination are age, stage of maturity and viability of the seeds, water, free supply of oxygen, and heat or temperature. A combination of most favourable conditions of these factors for each kind of seed is thus called the 'optimum' for that species.

If conditions are normal, most seeds will germinate with in a short time, but some may fail to do so because of immature embryos or a rest period or after-ripening period. Normally, an embryo has sufficient food material stored for germination, but in such isolated cased as the orchids, nutrients have to be provided externally to ensure germination.

The factors such as age, stage of, maturity and viability of seeds are inter-related. Viability of seeds determines their power to germinate. The poor viability of a seed may be due to the fact that it was harvested before full maturity or it might have been harvested from a weak plant and from plants grown under improper humidity and temperature. Viability also greatly depends upon the age of the seeds. Most of the annuals lose viability within 6 to 12 months. Seeds of some plants and trees should be sown immediately after 150 to 200 years.

Water is necessary since plant food should be made available to be embryo in a dissolved state. Moreover, water also softens the hard seed coat and hence encourages early seed germination. A quantity of water enough to completely saturate the seed coat should be used as too much watering is not good for germination. Excess of water may block the supply of oxygen or help the growth of disease-causing organism. On the other hand, some of the xerophytes and annuals such as Portulaca and eschscholtzia need small qualities of moisture for germination, whereas seeds of aquatics such as water lilies and lotus remain submerged.

The temperature should not be too high or too low. Some of the annuals such as nemophila and larkspur germinate better when the nights are really cool.

Light is not essential for germination for most of the species. Seeds of some species are indifferent to light, while others are slightly inhibited (*e.g.*, larkspur); some are completely or partially inhibited (*e.g.*, Nigella arvensis); still some others require light and geminate without cover (*e.g.*, members of Gesneriaceae, Ranuncululs, and Veronica).

Delayed Germination and Pre-treatment of Seeds

Some seeds do not geminate easily for a variety of reasons, the most common causes being dormancy, rest period, and presence of hard seed coat.

Seeds with hard coats require some kind of external treatments for germination (*e.g.*, seeds of palm and canna). The methods commonly employed are cracking of the coats by mechanical means, abrasion, soaking in water or acid, and stratification. Sulphuric acid (H_2SO_4) is often used at full, half, or one-fourth strength for periods varying from 10 to 30 min. Some seeds when soaked in water for 12 to 24 h or more germinate better. Stratification consists of fully exposing the seeds to the action of the weather by placing them in alternate layers of moist sand or sifted soil either in shallow boxes or in flats or in trenches outdoors. The flats and boxes are placed outdoors to be exposed to rain and snow and to freeze and thaw. In places not subjected to snowfall, the freezing treatments are given under artificial cold storage. The after-ripening period and the rest period can be shortened by treatment with low temperatures of 35° to 41°F for periods ranging from one to four months. Rose seeds are thus treated to got better germination. Larkspur also germinates better during the summer if stored in a cool moist place for several days before sowing.

Orchid seeds are so minute in size that they have very little or no stored food to nourish the growing embryo. Hence these are germinated in special media.

Seed Testing

Before sowing on a large-scale, it will be worthwhile to test the viability of the seeds. The simplest indoor method is, first, to sterilize by boiling in water or under pressure a paid of Petridishes and two piece of filter paper cut to size. Then one piece of filter paper is laid over the Petridish and the seeds spaced over it and the other piece is used to over the seeds. The filter papers are moistened with sterilized water and them the lid is put over this. The Petri dishes are kept in a dark, warm place. Some sterilized water may have to be supplied in between, till the seeds germinate. If most the seeds germinate, them it is assumed that the stock is of good viability.

(B) Vegetative Propagation

By vegetative propagation is meant the production of a complete plant from one vegetative bud or several such buds. This definition includes all asexual methods such as cutting, layering, division, separation, budding and grafting. Tissue culture method of propagation is also included.

Cutting

This may be defined as a process by which a plant is produced by severing a vegetative portion from the plant and rooting it in a favorable medium under optimum conditions. The plant parts that are used for this purpose are stems, toots leaves, and modified stems such as tubers, corms, rhizomes, runners, and bulbs. In general, propagation by cutting is the cheapest and the most convenient method and hence this is used more popularly to raise new plants. It is probably possible to raise most of the species of plants by one method of cutting or the other, but in the case of annuals, biennials, and some perennials some other methods such as seed age, layering and grafting are easier and more economical.

(1) Stem Cuttings

Stem cuttings are of three types (a) soft wood or herbaceous (b) semi-hard wood, and (c) hard wood. Experimental evidence shows that cuttings, with a few leaves at the top, root better than leafless cuttings.

(a) **Soft wood cuttings:** soft wood stem cuttings may again be separated into two distinct categories: (i) those taken from herbaceous plants such as carnation, chrysanthemum, coleus, dahlias, delphiniums, petunia *etc.* and (ii) the un ripened tips of woody plants such as most of the ornamental shrubs and some tees. Soft wood cuttings are taken from below a node and the bottom leaves are removed.

(b) **Semi-hard wood cuttings:** The portions of the stems which have passed the soft wood stage but re not yet nature are referred to as semi-hard wood cuttings. Semi-hard wood cuttings are used and the bottom leaves are removed.

(c) **Hard wood cuttings:** these are cuttings of shrubs and trees taken from mature current years growth. The length of cuttings varies with the type of plants and weather conditions. One meter to one and a half meters long hard wood cuttings of some trees and shrubs such as *Ficus benghalensis, Citharexylon, Gliricidia maculate,* and species of erythriana, when planted out in the open, root easily. But, generally, hard wood cuttings are 15 to 30 cm long. The soft wood or herbaceous cuttings are generally 2.5 cm to 10 cm long.

The water-shoots, which are over-vigorous and over-luxuriant growths from the base, do not make good cuttings. Similarly, in carnation the basal cuttings re not good, as these produce more vegetative growth than flowering. The cuttings of middle portions and tips are better in carnation. In some plants, the terminal tip cuttings produce better plants.

Stem Cuttings are of three Kinds

(i) **Terminal cuttings:** the lateral shoots which form the tip portion of the shoots. The lower leaves are removed by snipping (not tearing off) and only about four terminal leaves are left in such cuttings. If the terminal leaves are very large, they are cut to half of their length to minimize transpiration. Before inserting the succulent cuttings of cactus, cotyledon, *etc.*, these are allowed to dry up for 3-4 days or put in dry sand and not watered for a number of days.

(ii) **Heel cuttings:** The lateral shoots which re-pulled off from the stem and contain a portion of the stem are known as heel cuttings; these root more successfully than terminal cuttings, the rough wood and bark at the bottom may be smoothened with a sharp knife. Cuttings having a small portion of the woody branch attached to the base are similar to heel cuttings but are termed as mallet cuttings.

(iii) Node cuttings: Single or multiple node stem cuttings are also obtained from plants such as *Dieffenbachia* and *Dracaena* and these are inserted horizontally in sand.

With the present-day facilities such as mist propagation, propagation frames, bottom heat, *etc.*, it is possible to raise cuttings any time of the year. But, it has been found that the best time for taking cuttings corresponds to the time of the growing season of the parent plant. In most parts of India, the duration of this season is from July to September. In the hill stations, the corresponding the year.

All cuttings should be inserted fresh without delay except in cactus and some succulents. If there is a considerable time lag betw3een obtaining the cuttings and planting, these should be stored in shade, packed in either moist cloth or sphagnum moss. Instead of forcing the cutting through the medium, a hole of equal thickness should be made with the help of a stick and cutting inserted in the hole. The medium (soil, sand or vermiculite) around the cutting should be made firm to avoid failure.

Another important point is to insert in the rooting medium that end of the cutting which was nearest to the root of the parent plant. Root forms in a stem cutting at the end which is nearest to the root of the parent plant and shoot develops at the other end. This phenomenon is called 'polarity'. Sometimes a slanting cut below the node is given at the rooting end, thus exposing more tissue for callus formation. It is good for raising cuttings in earthen pot as this allows good aeration.

Soft-wood cuttings are inserted in the medium to a depth of 2.5 to 3 cm after removing the bottom leaves. The same procedure is followed for semi-hard wood cuttings. About one-third of the length of the cutting is inserted in the medium in the case of hard wood cuttings. Soft-wood and semi-hard wood cuttings are generally raised in partial shade, but the response to shading varies according to the season and the species. It has been observed that the shade provided by a muslin or cheese-cloth or roughly woven gunny cloth is good for an average plant. The grower will learn by experience the amount and the kind of shade needed for various plants during various seasons. When cutting are grown in a mist-chamber the need for shading becomes irrelevant. If planted other than in a mist-chamber the cuttings will need syringing 2-4 times a day depending on the weather. Hormones or growth substances play an important role in rooting of cuttings.

Rooting Media

A number of rooting media and their combinations have been suggested by various authors. A good rooting medium should be well aerated, but at the same time should hold enough moisture. While a wide range of plants toot well in alight soil, a large number of others need some special media or compost. The general practice is to use sterilized sharp sand, especially for soft wood or semi-hard wood cuttings, or a combination of sand and sphagnum peat. The use of sand alone as rooting medium is questioned by many and they suggest instead a mixture of sand and sphagnum peat especially for hard wood cuttings. Other media used for rooting medium is heated by bottom heat provided through fermenting manure, electricity or steam. In most parts of India, except in some hill stations, no bottom is needed.

Chapter 9

Graphics and Symbols in Landscape Design

In drawing a completed landscape design, designers use graphics and symbols, rather than words, to show many of the various components of the plan. Different graphics are used to indicate different types of plants, such as evergreens, deciduous trees, or groundcovers. Hardscape materials, such as brick, flagstone, and decking are also shown with different groups.

Graphic Language

It is a common experience, that when we read newspapers, magazines, leaflets, brochure, catalogues *etc.*, we grasp the information easily if it is illustrated with diagrams, sketches, pictures *etc.* Suppose an attempt is made to communication in writing the details of the shapes and sizes of the interior and exterior of a landscaping garden or a building in any language, it may become voluminous, and still may fail to convey the graphical and dimensional details precisely. However, by drawing one or more number of sketches of the landscaping, the details such as shapes and sizes of both its interior and exterior of garden can be conveyed precisely.

Graphic Language

The mode of communication through sketches is called graphic language.

Drawing

The graphical representation of an object is called drawing.

Landscape Drawing

To manufacture a component, or to develop a garden, both the shapes and sizes must be known before taking up the development. Therefore, the drawing of an object, which contains all the necessary information, like actual shape, accurate sizes, method of development, *etc.*, required for the development of an object is called landscape drawing.

Since, the landscaping of an object is drawn well before the object is constructed, the person who draws it must have a clear picture of the shape of the object. Since understanding of landscape drawing involves much of imagination, a systematic method is to be followed for its drawing and reading. Landscaping drawing may be either representational of graphic. The representation drawing shows only the appearance of an object, whereas the graphic drawing shows the accurate sizes and shapes of the object. Since landscape drawing is a graphical medium of expression of technical details without the barrier of a language, it is called the universal language of landscapers.

Drawing, Equipment and Instruments

Since the landscape drawing shows the accurate sizes and actual shapes of the object, it must be drawn to scale with the aid of geometrical instruments. A brief study of the necessary drawing equipment and instruments, and the proper method of using them are made here.

Drawing Board

The drawing board is made of well seasoned pine wood. This is rigid, sturdy and light in weight. Along the left edge of the board, a groove is cut, and a perfectly supporting guide for the T-square to slide on. The drawing board must be placed on the table with the working edge always to be at the left side. The standard sizes of the drawing boards recommended by the Bureau of Indian Standards, ISI: 1444-1963 are given in Table 4.1. In drawing officers, first two sizes are used and for students use D 2 size is convenient.

Table 4.1: Dimensions of Engineer's Drawing Boards (Dimensions in mm)

Designation	*Length × Width*	*Recommended for Use with Sheet Sizes*
D0	1500 x 1000	A0
D1	1000 x 700	A1
D2	700 x 500	A2
D3	500 x 350	A3

T-square

The T-square is made of well seasoned hard wood and consists of two parts namely blade and stock. The stock slides over the working edge of the drawing board. The blade which moves on the surface of the board has a drawing edge. The drawing edge is beveled and in some type of T-squares it is made of transparent plastic edge so that the immediate next line covered by it will visible. Its main use is to draw horizontal lines and also it serves as a support to place the set-square over it.

Set-square

Generally, these are available in pairs. One is 60° – 30° set square and another is 45° set-square. These are used to draw vertical, inclined and parallel lines and for setting the combination of the angles in multiples of 15°.

Protractor

This is made of celluloid. Protractor will be either semicircular or circular. It is used to set up or measure any given angle.

Clinograph

This is used to draw a series of parallel and perpendicular lines.

Drafting Machine and Mini-drafter

A drafting machine is used by professional draftsman to produce the drawings with ease and rapidity. It combines all the functions of the T-square, set-square, protractor and clinograph. A simplified miniature version of the drafting machine called 'mini-drafter'. It consists of a clamp provided with a screw, two pairs of parallelogram of bars, a protractor head with a screwed knob, and two mutually perpendicular metallic or celluloid scales with ruling edges. The two pairs of parallelogram of bars are provided at right angles to a pivot place. One pair of parallelogram of bars is pivoted to the clamp while the other pair is pivoted to the protractor, which can be swiveled to any angular position. The knob provided at the protractor head facilities the clamping of the scales in any angular position.

Pencils

Two types of pencils used in engineering drawing practice are:

(i) Wooden pencils, and

(ii) Mechanical clutch pencils.

(i) Wooden Pencil

Wooden pencils are graded and designated by the numbers and letters from 6B, very soft and black through, 5B, 4B, 3B, 2B, B in the decreasing order of softness and blackness, and HB to F, the medium grade then H, 2H, 3H, 4H, 5H, 6H, 7H, 8H, 9H in the increasing order of hardness. For students use, H, 2H and HB pencils and finished with H or HB pencils.

(ii) Mechanical Clutch Pencil

Mechanical clutch pencils with 0.5mm thick lead are preferred than the wooden pencils as they need no sharpening. H, 2H and HB grade leads are used in these pencils.

French Curves

French curves are templates of various curved-shapes. The French-curve is used as a guiding edge for drawing non-circular curves. First, sufficient number of points on the curve to be drawn is determined. A smooth continuous freehand curve is drawn passing through all the points. Then place the French curves selecting a part of it that will fit with the portion of the curve, draw only that portion of the curve using the French curve as guiding edge. Next shift the French Curves to find its portion that will fit to continue the next portion of the curve.

Drawing Pins or Clips or Tape

These are used to secure the drawing sheets to the drawing board firmly. The use of pins must be avoided, as it will spoil the surface of the board. The cellophane tape strips are widely used instead of drawing pins and clips.

Eraser

Soft rubber is the widely used form of eraser.

Erasing Shield

It is a thin plastic or metallic plate cut with slots of different lengths, widths and shapes, used to erase unwanted pencil lines without erasing the surrounding lines.

Drawing Instrument Box

The instrument box consists of a compass with interchangeable pencil or pen legs, a divider, a bow-divider and a lengthening bar.

Scales

Scales are the measuring devices usually made either of cardboard or plastic. They are available in a set consisting of eight-scales, designated from M1 to M8. The standard recommended scales to be used in engineering drawing are given in Table 4.2.

Table 4.2: Standard Recommended Scales

Designation		*Scale*
M_1	Full size	1:1
	50cm to a meter	1:2
M_2	40cm to a meter	1:1.25
	20cm to a meter	1:5
M_3	10cm to a meter	1:10
	5cm to a meter	1:20
M_4	2cm to a meter	1:50
	1cm to a meter	1:100
M_5	5mm to a meter	1:200
	2mm to a meter	1:500
M_6	0.33cm to a meter	1:300
	0.66cm to a meter	1:600
M_7	0.25mm to a meter	1:400
	0.125mm to a meter	1:800
M_8	1mm to a meter	1:1000
	0.5mm to a meter	1:2000

Drawing Sheets

The standard sizes of the drawing sheets recommended by the Bureau of Indian Standards are given in below Table 4.3. The surface area of A0 size sheet is one square meter. The sizes of the successive drawing sheets are obtained by halving the previous higher size sheet. The widths to length ratio for all sheet sizes are maintained as 1:2. A2 size drawing sheet is convenient for students use.

Table 4.3: Standard Size of Drawing Sheets

Designation	*Length x Width*
A0	841 x 1489
A1	594 x 841
A2	420 x 594
A3	297 x 420
A4	210 x 297

All dimensions in mm.

Layout of Drawing Sheets

The layout of a drawing sheet is the standard form of arrangement of the important particulars which are shown on it to ensure that all the necessary information is included in the drawing sheet and facilitate its quick reading and to make it possible for essential references to be located easily, especially when drawings are prepared by several officers.

Positioning of Drawing Sheets

The drawing sheets may be positioned with their longer sides being placed either horizontally or vertically depending on overall sizes of the drawing to be drawn.

Borders

The border is the space left all round in between the trimmed edges of the drawing sheet and the frame. It has been recommended that these borders have a minimum width of 20 mm for A0 and A1 sizes, and a minimum width of 10 mm for A2, A3 and A4 sizes.

Filing Margin

A filing margin may be provided for taking perforations. This margin shall have a minimum width of 20 mm with the border included therein.

Grid Reference System

A grid reference system is provided for all the sizes of drawing sheets to facilitate easy location of any portion of the drawing within the frame. The length and width of the frames are divided into even number of divisions. The number of divisions chosen for a particular sheet depends on the complexity of the drawing.

Tile Block

A title block is an important feature provided on a technical drawing or with an associated document for recording the technical and administrative details. It is placed on the right hand bottom corner of the drawing sheet. The space in the title block is divided into:

(*i*) Identification zone

(*ii*) Additional information zone.

The identification zone includes the following basic information:

☆ Registration or identification number

- Title of the drawing
- The name of the legal owner of the drawing, *i.e.*, name of the firm or the company

The additional information zone includes the following items:

- Indicative items
- Technical items
- Administrative items

Indicative Items

The symbol indicating the system of projection employed for the drawing, the main scale of the drawing, and the linear unit of the dimension if it is other than the millimeter.

Technical Items

Method of indicating the surface texture, method of indicating the geometric tolerances, values of general tolerances and the other relevant standards.

Method of Numbering the Multiple Sheet Drawings

If more than one sheet is required for a component or an assembly, then the same registration or identification number must be indicated by means of a sequential sheet number. In addition, the total number of sheets should be shown on sheet 1, for example, Sheet No. n/p.

Where, **n** is the sequential sheet number and **p** is the total number of sheets.

Instruments required for measurements

1. Measuring tape
2. Cross stop
3. Ranging rod
4. Pegs and bars

Landscape (Garden) Symbols

Garden symbols are nothing but the pictures, which are used for representing the various garden components (features). They are mainly used in preparing the garden plan or design. The symbols cover primarily the garden surfaces such as steps, different types of shrubs, trees, climbers, perennials and other plants. On plan, the symbols are drawn to scale wherever possible and make the transition from broad outline plan to detailed structural and planting plans. When drawing symbols, generally it should look as much as possible like the shape of the plant or structure it is representing.

Chapter 10

Landscape Design

The selection of suitable tools/implements is essential for carrying out various horticultural operations. For example several tools are there for cutting branches of plants such as secature, tree pruner, pruning saw, carpenter's saw *etc.* If the thickness of branch is about 1-2 cm, the secature may be more suitable, similarly if the branch in 4-6 cm is thickness pruning saw is the proper tool, and if the branch is still bigger (more than 8cm) carpenter's saw may be required. Therefore one has to exercise option to select a suitable tool/implement to carryout various operations from the stage of land preparation to harvesting.

The tools, implements and plant protection equipments are commonly used in the horticultural crops are given in Table 5.1

Table 5.1: Tools/Implement/Plant-Protection Equipments that are Used in Horticultural Crops

Sl.No.	*Tools/Implement/Plant-Protection Equipments*	*Uses in Landscaping*
1.	Automizer	For spraying nursery beds, potted plants *etc.*
2.	Axe	For felling the trees
3.	Back sak sprayer	For spraying nursery beds, flowerbeds, potted plants *etc.*
4.	Bill hook	To cut the bigger stems near the ground surface
5.	Bolo-power sprayer	For spraying plant protection chemicals on large areas.
6.	Budding-cum-grafting knife	For both grafting and budding. It has two sharp blades to give cuts on the stock and scion and the back end (flap) made up of plastic or brass used to lift or loosen the bark for inserting the bud.

Sl.No.	Tools/Implement/Plant-Protection Equipments	Uses in Landscaping
7.	Carpenter's saw	To prune the bigger branches, (more than 8cm diameter) it is specially useful in crown grafting
8.	Crow-bar	An iron rod of 4-6 ft in length with one end pointed and the other end flattened. Used for digging pits and moving rocks
9.	Dibbler	To make small holes on the seed beds in order to place seeds or transplant seedlings.
10.	Digging fork	To loosen the moist soil or manure pits.
11.	Drainage hoe	To make the drainage channel and to remove silt deposit in the channels.
12.	Dutch hoe	To loosen the surface soil between the rows of plants for removing small weeds.
13.	Foot Sprayer	Requires two labours for operation.
14.	Forester's shear	To prune the medium sized branches (4-8cm) which are at higher height on the trees.
15.	Garden hand rake	For removing stubbles, small stones, leveling of nursery beds and formation of small beds
16.	Garden trowel/shovel	For lifting more number of seedlings.
17.	Grass shear	To cut the out growth of grasses planted in posts, carpet beds
18.	Hand cultivator	To loosen the soil, remove clods, pebbles in nursery beds and mixing of manures and fertilizers.
19.	Hand fork	To loosen the soil in seedbeds and to break the clods.
20.	Hand guddali	For light digging and other intercultural operations.
21.	Hand Rotary Duster	For dusting the powdery chemicals on plants.
22.	Hand sprayer	For spraying potted plants
23.	Hatchet	To remove or cut down the bigger stems and broken stems
24.	Hedge shear	To prune the tender parts of garden shear the plants, it is specially useful for trimming hedges, borders, topiary work
25.	Hose pipe	To irrigate flower beds, lawns *etc.*
26.	Knapsack sprayer	For spraying nursery beds, flower beds, potted plants *etc.*
27.	Kurpi-Varvari	For weeding and stirring the soil in the pots and beds.
28.	Lawn mower	To cut the grass uniformly in the lawn. It is having a roller behind to pad the grass to have cushion.
29.	Lawn sprinkler	For irrigating lawns.
30.	Pick Axe	For light digging and loosening the soil
31.	Pick-axe	For opening trenches, channels, digging pits, loosening soil *etc.*
32.	Pruning knife	For pruning of thicker branches and it has curved knife.
33.	Pruning saw	To prune the thicker branches (4-6cm girth) of an acute crotch (angle).
34.	Pruning shear	For cutting small sized branches.
35.	Rocker sprayer (Gattar)	For spraying plant protection chemicals particularly in plantations/ orchards

Sl.No.	Tools/Implement/Plant-Protection Equipments	Uses in Landscaping
36.	Rotary weeder	For cutting of grasses in lawn, carpet beds, edges *etc.*
37.	Scythe (Dabba)	For cutting lawn grasses, vegetables *etc.*
38.	Secature	To prune the branches, twigs, water suckers *etc.* of small plants.
39.	Seed Trays (Plastic)	Used for sowing seeds prior to planting out
40.	Sickle	For cutting grasses, vegetables *etc.*
41.	Sieve	Used for removing small stones from soil
42.	Spade	To loosen the soil, prepare irrigation channels, collect the soil in heaps and facilitate filling up of soil, manure *etc.* in the baskets.
43.	Transplanting trowel	To lift the young seedlings along with a boll of earth for transplanting.
44.	Tree calipers	To measure the girth of trees trunks.
45.	Tree pruner	To cut down the smaller branches of the trees without climbing.
46.	Trenching hoe	For light collection of soil, irrigation purposes and opening of trenches.
47.	Water can with rose head	To water the young seedling in seed beds, potted plants *etc.* the rose head facilitates with fine spray of water which prevents the washing down of soil.
48.	Weed cutters	Special kinds of weed cutter have a serrated double edged steel blade and handle about 60cm long. It is used with swinging strokes in two directions.
49.	Wheel barrow	To transport manures, soil, seedlings, garden waste *etc.*

Chapter 11

Layout of Styles of Gardens

The historical development of gardens in various countries during ancient period had set different styles of gardening which were influenced by environmental factors, as well as by the people and their functions and purpose, such as for pleasure, comfort, grandeur or display of social status. The gardens of antiquity created in the Far East and Asia Minor, China, Babylon, Persia, Egypt and Greece were associated with *villas*, palaces and house of kings. The Hanging Gardens of Babylon became one of the seven wonders of the old world. During 16th and 17th centuries, flowers dominated the gardens developed in Italy and other European countries. The garden styles have been classified. The two most common garden styles based on form and shape are the formal and informal garden styles.

Formal Gardens

A formal garden is laid out in a symmetrical or a geometrical pattern. In this garden the design is stiff as everything is done in a straight and narrow way. In such gardens everything is planted in straight lines. Also if there is a plant on the left hand side of a straight road, a similar plant must be planted at the opposite place on the right hand side *i.e.*, mirror image of each other. The flower beds, borders, and shrubbery are arranged in geometrically designed beds. Trimmed formal hedges, Cypress, *Ashoka* trees, and topiary are typical features of a formal garden, *e.g.*, Mughal, Persian, Italian and French styles of gardens.

Informal Gardens

In an informal garden, the whole design looks informal, as the plans and the features are arranged in a natural way without following any hard and fast rules. But here also the work has to proceed according to a set and well-through-out plan; otherwise the creation will not be artistic and attractive. The idea behind this design is to imitate nature. *e.g.*, English and Japanese gardens

Wild Garden

A comparatively recent style of gardening, namely, 'Wild Garden' was expounded by William Robinson in the last decade of the nineteenth century. His idea was revolutionary and found many admirers to follow this. The concept of wild garden is not only against all formalism but it also breaks the rule of landscape styles.

The points to be in mind while developing this type of garden are:

1. Naturalize plants in shrubberies
2. Grass should remain unmowed as in nature with few bulbous plants grown scattered in the grass to imitate wild scenery.
3. Creepers to be allowed to grow over the trees naturally imitating those of the forests.

Mr. William Robinson also suggested that passages should be opened in the woodland, and trees, shrubs, and bulbous plants should be planted among the forest flora to fulfill his idea of a wild garden. His other idea was to allow the creepers to grow over the trees naturally imitating those of the forests.

Before someone starts to venture into designing a garden it will be wise to get an idea abut the major gardening styles of the world. This will pen up a window to this knowledge on gardening and help him design his own garden by adapting the best from each or any of these. But this does not mean that one should copy any garden style. For instance, when a person studies Shakespeare, Shaw, or Tagore it does not mean that one will translate their ideas in his work of literature. One only studies the styles of writing and forms his own ideas suiting to the situation and time. Similarly, a garden enthusiast has to study the different styles only to gain knowledge to help him form his own ideas suiting the local condition and limitations such as a available space, funds, *etc.*

Different Garden Styles

Free Style Garden

This style of gardening combines the good features of formal and informal designs. The example for this type of garden is the rose garden at Ludhiana in Punjab.

Though in India from history and ancient literature we find that gardening was quite in vogue in olden times, but unfortunately there is no garden style called 'Indian garden', which can claim a place in the major gardening styles of the world. The famous garden style of India the 'Mughal Gardens' is nothing but a replica of the ancient Persian Gardens.

The Hindu Styles of Gardens

Vanams in the earlier period served the purpose of a garden and was synonymous with garden. Vanams were the natural gardens furnished by the mother earth for the human being and animals to dwell on and inhabit in. Such vanams were put to various uses by the various sections of the society. Vanavasam was part of the life of Vikrmaditya, Rama and Pandavas. The great sages reside only in vanams to attain spiritual bliss.

Rajavanam

Area of natural forest exclusively meant for kings to hunt wild animals. More than hunting, it was the time spent in hunting that is relaxing in real sense. Latter on four kinds of Rajavanams came into existence.

(*i*) **Promododyan**: Private garden for king and queen exclusively. It would get attached to the forts where queen resided.

(*ii*) **Udayan**: A vanam where the kings passed their leisure time in playing chess, enjoying dance and listening to music.

(*iii*) **Vriksha vatica**: a vanam meant for ministers and courtiers where they made merry with courtesans.

(*iv*) Special gardens dedicated to god with water pools studded with lotuses and lilies.

Tabovanam

It was meant for sages and hermits who would proper to be intone with nature and meditate to explore the self and the universal god head. Tabovanams would have the trees of spiritual significance.

(*i*) *Guttardia speciosa* (Panneer)

(*ii*) *Couropita guinensis* (Nagalingam)

(*iii*) *Butea frondosa* (Vedic tree-real flame of the forest)

(*iv*) *Callophyllum inophyllum* (Punnai)

(*v*) *Michelia champaca* (Sanbakam)

(*vi*) *Ficus benghalensis* (To fulfill all human dosiles)

Brindavanam

It means a place of eternal bliss. It is supposed to be the advanced version of *tabovanam*. It is a natural abode where the sages relinquish their physical body and attain radiant body (*Nirvikalpa Samadhi*) and the soul part of the body conjoints with the absolute. God head in eternal ectacy, *e.g.*, Arvind Ashram, Pudducherry, Mantralayam of Ragavendra, Ramana and Seshadri brindavans at Tiruvannamalai. Trees with showy, colourfull flowers to express the absolute joy would be grown in Brindavans.

Asokavanam

It was a place or a garden where royal ladies like queens and princess relax. Asoka trees (*Saraca indica*) were grown in woodlots. The down flowing coppery leaves of *saraca* would suggest to royal ladies that their kings would return with triumph and passify their emotionally imbalanced heart.

Nandavanams

They are small gardens established around village temples. There the flowering shrubs whose flowers can be offered to various deities are grown for daily rituals *e.g., Tauberna Montana coronana, Hibiscus, Tecoma, Nerium, Sanctum sanctorium, jasmines*

Indus and Harappan Civilization

The history of systematic gardening in India is as old as civilization of Indus and Harappan which existed between 2500 *BC* and 1750 *BC*.

- ☆ Harappan pots were generally decorated with designs of tress – *pipal,* mango and neem.
- ☆ The cult of animal and tree worship was at its peak.
- ☆ The tree of *pipal* (*Ficus celigiosa*) and banyan (*Ficus bengalensis*) served mankind and fauna in many different ways and they were considered as the symbol of fertility.

Aryavartha Period

It existed during 1600 *BC*. Aryavartha means the country of lotus and sunshine. Lotus signifies the soul and the sun signifies the godheads. The blooming lotus on the radiating sun's arms symbolizes the ultimate purpose of human life, *i.e.* the soul's unification with God.

- ☆ They were ardent lovers of nature.
- ☆ They used flowers for religious and social ceremonies.
- ☆ They named the kids after the flowers *e.g.,* Kamal Chanbagam, Madhavi, Chameli, Rukmani and Mallika.

Chapter 12

Layout of Informal Gardens

An informal garden is naturalistic and usually includes asymmetrically placed design elements, naturally shaped plants and beds, curved spaces, rustic-looking furnishings, and more casual pavings, like decking and even wood chips. It can be flowery and colorful or low key to suit the personality of the gardener. Most gardens, particularly larger ones, feature elements of both the formal and informal styles.

Among the different styles of gardening in the world, the English and Japanese gardens are categories as informal gardens.

The English Gardens

The English landscape garden, also called English landscape park or simply the English garden, is a style of 'landscape' garden which emerged in England in the early 18th century, and spread across Europe, replacing the more formal, symmetrical of the 17th century as the principal gardening style of Europe. The English gardens are most beautiful among all European gardens. The main idea used in English gardens was that the gardens should merge with the countryside without any artificial barriers such as fences, hedges *etc.* Due to favorable climatic conditions such as high annual rainfall, the natural ground cover in the English countryside is grass. With this in mind the famous British garden architects Repton and Capaciblity Brown advocated the concept that the British gardens should like the countryside. Their main idea was that the gardens should merge with the countryside without any artificial barriers such as fences, hedges, or the like. But it is only in the eighteenth century that these two gentlemen along with Kent brought the touch of nature in the garden, although the history of gardening in England dates back of fourteenth century. They started kitchen gardens to supply vegetables to the inmates of the monasteries and grew herb gardens for medicines. But this gradually imbibed the spirit of gardening to the people who realized the goodness of residing in pleasant surroundings. By the middle of the sixteenth century the English gardens saw flower beds, topiary, and terrace gardens. In the middle of the eighteenth century gardens were laid out with more emphasis on architectural features. The main features of gardens during this period were curved paths, informal groups of trees, rivulets or streams, artificial waterfalls, and clipped hedges. The flowering annuals, the main stay of an English garden, came into prominence during the nineteenth century which subdued the architectural features.

About the English Garden

History of gardening in England started from 14th century. In 16th century – idea of flower beds, topiary, terrace gardens was implemented in the gardens. The English in 18th century completely changed the idea of garden with nature. Idea of gardening was given by British garden architects Capability Brown along with Kent. They produced naturalistic garden in contrast to the rigidity and formality seen in formal gardens. Alexander Pope, Claude Lorraine, Nicholas Poussin were some of the artists at that time who influenced a lot for gardening. Mid 18th century – more emphasis was given to architectural features.

Charles Howard (1699) engaged Mr. John Vanburgh which consisted of various architectural elements and sculptural figures.

William Kent (1730) showed a garden style which was a mixture of formal and informal style. Created rolling fields and placed water at the site of the temples to see the reflections of temple in the lake.

Henry Hoare (1740) designed Stourhead which an example of the estate designed by him. His landscape design was greatly influenced by Claude Lorraine paintings. Hoare designed a prescribed path.Whole circuit around the lake took visitors through numerous structures.

The main features of an English garden are the lawn, mixed border especially of herbaceous annuals, as well as herbaceous perennials, shrubbery, and rock gardens. The English climate suit admirably well for the growth of herbaceous annuals. This prompted them to evolve a large number of hybrids of annuals as well as to collect the best flowering plants from all over the world. Most of the flowering annuals that we see today in the Indian gardens, with the few exceptions of amaranthus, balsam, Gomphrena, marigold, *etc.*, were brought here by the British.

Some of the important English gardens are:

1. Royal Botanical Garden, Kew

Established in 1757 AD with the establishment of Royal Horticultural Society in 1804 AD, the royal pleasure gardens at Kew assumed the role of botanical gardens. Vast number of plants from abroad were brought and maintained. 'Hortus Kewensis' a catalogue of plants cultivated at Kew was published in 1789 AD. Later on many new inventions were made and by 1861 AD lake garden were completed. Rock garden and water gardens were also made. Plants like rhododendron and orchids from India and chrysanthemum, lilies, and cherries from Japan brought revolution in English gardens.

2. Chelsea Physic Garden

Every year there is a great spring show for 4 days in May, organised by Royal Horticultural Society. This show has been held at the Royal Hospital Chelsea's grounds since 1913 which covers the area of 11 hectares. The Royal Horticultural Society renders free guidance to gardener of every degree.

3. Cottage Gardens

These are the small gardens made around cottages of lower and middle class people. Fruit trees and vegetables including potatoes are grown in abundance. Hedges and topiary are common features along with fragrant annuals like sweet William, pinks, lavender, tulip *etc.* arranged in herbaceous border and roses of different classes.

The Japanese Gardens

The Japanese gardens are more of traditional that create miniature idealized landscapes, often in a highly abstract and stylized way. The gardens of the Emperors and nobles were designed for recreation and aesthetic pleasure, while the gardens of Buddhist temples were designed for contemplation and meditation.

Both the Persian and Japanese garden designs were based on their respective ideas of heaven. One most admirable feature of the Japanese garden is that while other major styles of gardening of the world changed radically or fallen into dis-flavour, the Japanese continued the same style for centuries but still remained popular. This can be attributed to the special relation of the Japanese gardens to nature.

A most important teaching of the Japanese garden is possibly that "unless a garden has an air of peace it's not worth a place visiting. It should be a place where the mind finds rest and relaxation." The Japanese gardens which are planned with so much of thought appear so casual that they do not appeal to many people.

Another strong basis of the Japanese garden is its immutability, *i.e.*, except some seasonal changes in the deciduous trees the Japanese garden hardly goes through any other strong visible changes during different seasons. Even during the winter the Japanese gardens have their own beauty with snow flakes hanging down the stone pieces or the stone lanterns. The immutability is achieved also because rather than a grand mixture of flowers, shrubs, and trees more emphasis is placed on natural elements such as a simple path, a group of rocks, stepping stones, streams, waterfalls, bridges, stone lanterns, and so on. A Japanese garden tries to capture natural scenery or to imitate a landscape. The three elements most important to achieve these objectives are water, stone, and plants. Low sculptured bushes and trained dwarfed trees look very attractive in a Japanese garden.

Some of the important Japanese Gardens include Kenroku en in Kanazawa, Koraku-en in Okayama and Kairaku-en in Mito.

Kenroku-en in Kanazawa

Kenroku-en was developed from the 1620s to the 1840s by the Maeda clan, the daimyo who ruled the former Kaga Domain. It is located in Kanazawa, Ishikawa, Japan, is an old private garden. This garden contains roughly 8,750 trees, and 183 species of plants in total. Among the garden's points of special interest are

a. The oldest fountain in Japan, operating by natural water pressure.[10]
b. Yûgao-tei, a teahouse, the oldest building in the garden, built 1774
c. Shigure-tei, a rest House that was originally built by the 5th lord Tsunanori, reconstructed at its present location in 2000
d. Karasaki Pine, planted from seed by the 13th lord Nariyasu from Karasaki, near Lake Biwa.
e. Kotoji-tôrô, a stone lantern with two legs, said to resemble the bridge on a koto. This lantern is emblematic of Kenroku-en and Kanazawa.
f. Flying Geese Bridge (Gankô-bashi), made of eleven red stones, laid out to resemble geese in a flying formation
g. Kaiseki Pagoda, said to have been donated to the Maeda by Toyotomi Hideyoshi

In winter, the park is notable for its yukitsuri — ropes attached in a conical array to carefully support tree branches in the desired arrangements, thereby protecting the trees from damage caused by heavy snows.

Kôraku-en

This garden is located in Okayama, Okayama Prefecture and was built in 1700 by Ikeda Tsunamasa, lord of Okayama. The garden covers a total area of approximately 133,000 square meters, with the grassed area covering approximately 18,500 square meters. During 1687, begin to construct the garden. It was completed in 1700. The garden is located on the north bank of the Asahi River on an island between the river and a developed part of the city. The garden has many features including the lawns, ponds, hills, tea houses, and streams.The length of the stream which runs through the garden is 640 meters. It features a central pond called Sawa-no-ike (Marsh Pond), which contains three islands purported to replicate the scenery around Lake Biwa near Kyoto.

Kairaku-en

This Japanese garden located in Mito, Ibaraki, Japan. Kairakuen was built relatively recently in the year 1841 by the local lord Tokugawa Nariaki. This garden served not only for the enjoyment of the ruling lord, but was open to the public. While worth a visit throughout the year, Kairakuen is most attractive during the plum blossom season, which usually takes place in late February and March. Besides the plum tree forest, where one hundred different plum tree varieties with white, pink and red blossoms are planted, Kairakuen also features a bamboo grove, cedar woods and the Kobuntei, a traditional Japanese style building.

Types of Garden

A Japanese garden may either be in the form of a large public park or a small family garden designed for living which is seen usually by members of the family or the family guests. The Japanese gardens are further classified based on positions, shape, and purpose. The important types are:

1. Hill garden
2. Fat garden,
3. Tea garden,
4. Passage garden, and
5. Sand gardens.

(1) Hill Garden

Out of the various styles, this one is considered to be the ideal by many garden enthusiasts. This style is known in Japanese as 'Tsukiyama-niwa or Tsukiyama-sansui', meaning hills and water. The hill garden is made up of one or more hills designed with earth mounds and exposed weathered stones. The other features of this garden area water in the form of a stream or a pond or waterfalls or all the three with or without islands and also bridges, lantern, stones, and trees. The important points in the garden are decorated with stones and selected trees. But pine trees may be planted to give the effect of being swept by wind. Untrimmed stepping stones are placed over the walks.

An island is generally a usual feature in a hill garden. When the island is present it should be decorated with a "Worshipping stone", called raithai-seki in Japanese, a "Sow-viewing" lantern and a pine tree.

(2) Flat Garden

As the name implies, *Hira-niwa* or flat gardens are laid out in flat ground without hills or ponds. Flat gardens are supposed to represent a mountain valley or a meadowland. These gardens were popular during the era of Muromachi.

A Fat garden is not necessarily as flat as a pan-cake. Since it stimulates a mountain valley, low rounded hills designed with the help of stones or earth mounds or both will look quite appropriate in a flat garden. But some others opine that there should not be any ups and downs in a flat garden.

The usual features to break the monotony of a flat garden are a well, a water-basin made of stone in the shape of an urn, stones lying close to the ground. In a flat garden, the principle is to avoid strong vertical lines represented by tall pines.

(3) Tea Garden

The tea garden is laid out based on certain principles and customs of the Japanese tea ceremony and hence needs a considerable space of at least about 200 square metres, for its designing. Since the performance of the tea ceremony needs an atmosphere of intimacy it is essential that the garden be enclosed by a fence. But the fence should be rustic in mature, with a gate made of very light material such as bamboo.

To protect the tea house from the noise of the outer world, the tea gardens are divided into an outer garden (*soto-roji*) and inner garden (*uchi-roji*).

The outer tea garden is comparatively a narrow area, with a waiting place where the guests are supposed to wait until the master of the house appears to welcome them. This waiting place has a water-basin for the convenience of the guests who can wash their hands and a stone lantern for illumination, but in present days this serves more as a decoration piece. A stone path, usually of stepping-stones, leads to the inner garden. The inner garden is also separated from the outer garden by a rustic fence and a gate made of light material.

The inner garden contains the tea house. The tea house of the classical time was nothing but a small straw hut with an outside waiting place, a small side room for washing the utensils, and the main ceremonial tea house itself having a capacity to accommodate only five persons. The entire path to the tea house is paved with stones or studded with stepping-stone.

The most important feature at the entrance of the tea house is a water-basin or a well or both for the visitors to rinse their face before entering for the tea ceremony. To illuminate the water basin and resting place stone lanterns are set in appropriate places. The selection of water-basin and stone lanterns is done with scrupulous care so that both the purposes of utility and beauty and elegance are fulfilled.

As far as tree planting is concerned, a contrast is maintained between the outer garden and the inner garden. The outer garden will have simple plantings and stone groupings. The outer garden should be exposed to sun and hence planting of deciduous trees should predominate. The inner garden is a subdued area and hence evergreen trees casting more shadows are used here.

The entrance to the tea house is through a low-door so that the guests have to enter in a bending posture, simulating respect and humility.

(4) Passage Garden

The passage gardens, the *Roji-niwa*, are those which are laid in narrow passage, as for example a narrow space between two houses or approaches to buildings. As such areas are generally narrow, the garden lay-out should be simple and not over crowded.

In such gardens there should be hardly any ornaments such as lanterns, basins or other man-made features. The common features of a passage garden are a few key rocks, slabs of stones, and only a couple of types of plant. Bushy shrubs and trees are unsuitable in a passage garden; instead, plants with open form and slender shapes are selected.

The passage gardens generally occur as an accidental necessity in a narrow passage formed by two buildings of a large property. But, occasionally a narrow passage is purposively created to simulate a distant prospect.

(5) Sand Garden

It is the simplest style of gardening, though not liked by many as it is totally devoid of plants. The most famous sand garden exists in Kyoto and is known as Ryoanji garden. The garden consists of a rectangular area of about 350 square metres adjoining a Zen Budhist temple.

The main feature of this style of gardening is to arrange few vertical and prostrate stones in groups of 2 or 3 and to fill in gap between the stones with fine white gravel. The gravel is raked in most simple patterns simulating the ripples of flowing water. The raking has to be repeated often to keep the garden in its best shape. This style of garden looks pleasant and effective only when confined to a limited area.

The Features of Japanese Gardens

(a) Ponds

The geometric shape does not live up to the Japanese tradition and hence all ponds are of irregular shape. The banks are generally bordered with stone piling work in a regular or an irregular fashion. In olden days the bottom used to be made impervious by puddling clay. But now-a-days concrete-bottomed ponds are also used. The ponds are generally fed by a stream or a waterfall.

(b) Streams

Small streams in Japanese gardens are arranged most naturally with natural stones bordering the banks. Often fanciful stones are arranged in midstream to break the flow of water. The flow of water in the stream may be manipulated by changing the inclination. Sometimes it may be as fast as a mountain rivulet or like a smooth-flowing river of the plains.

(c) Waterfalls

The presence of waterfalls in Japanese gardens is another attempt in imitating nature. A waterfall may be made more effective by manipulating it to drop in two or three levels. To make the waterfalls dignified and natural, large-sized stones are arranged around these. For many Japanese, the naked exposer of the cascade of water is not to good taste and hence these are partially screened by planting a group of trees in front of the waterfall. The dense planting of evergreens around the waterfall also symbolizes mountain scenery where actually a waterfall naturally belongs.

(d) Fountains

Often natural fountains are provided near the foot of the hill, on the hillside or in the forest. Often water is conveyed from a hillside by means of bamboo-piping.

(e) Wells

In olden days wells in the garden were features of utility. In modern times this feature is more in the nature of an ornament than a utility. The wells may be square, circular, or criss-cross in shape. The frame is generally constructed of stone but occasionally wood is also used. The frame is generally raised above the ground level to a height of 45-60 cm, The mouth of the well is often covered with a mat or a flexible lid knitted out of bamboo-square-shaped buckets are hung on either side of the pulley, suspended from a rope. The well must be made very ornamental.

(f) Islands

There are **four important garden islands**, the first two types representing sea islands.

1. **"Elysian Isle" (Horai-jima)** which is constructed in the middle of a lake and is never connected by a bridge. The beach is decorated with sand from the sea, shells, and pebbles. No fresh water vegetation is planted over this island. Often this island is given the shape of a tortoise.
2. "**Wind'swept Isle" (Fukiagae-jima),** is also an ocean isle and constructed in a similar way. In addition to sand and shell, the beaches here are decorated with sea rocks.
3. **"Master's Isle" (Shujin-to)** - is placed in the foreground of the landscape so that it can be easily approached by a bridge from the bank. The "Master's Isle" generally has a summer house which is nothing but a thatched arbour. Besides the arbour, some selected trees, stones, stepping-stones, and one or two lanterns are included. Often the islands are in the shape of mounds or hillocks. Often the islands are made a peninsula, connected to the mainland by a narrow neck of land instead of a bridge.
4. **"Guest's Isle (Kiakujin-to)-** is located in the background and is accessible by bridges and stepping-stones.

(g) Bridges

These are a special feature in a Japanese garden. These are used to reach an island or for crossing a stream. Bridges may be made of stones, polished or unworked earth, wood, and other materials. The main criterion is that the construction should be pleasing to the eye. The Japanese concept of a bridge is not just a quick crossing of a water way. The aim is to prolong the crossing time so that the visitor gets enough time to enjoy the scenery around. Even when slabs of stones are used as a bridge, one single span will not connect the destination, but there will be a detour in the midstream and another slab running in a different direction will carry the visitor to the ultimate point.

The earthen bridge is constructed by first putting a wooden framework over which bundles or small logs are laid across and then these are covered with about 15 to 20 cm layer of earth and gravel.

Often to cross a marshy place or a stream a bridge called Yatsu-hashi is constructed by placing eight wooden plants in a zig-zag manner supported by arched beams raising from the riverbed. A combination of stepping-stones and bridges is also often used to reach an island or to cross a stream. If there are two or more bridges in the garden, different types should be constructed to bring variety. When the pond or waterway is large enough to permit boating, the bridges should be arching type to permit the boats to pass under.

(h) Water Basins

The water-basins are fitted near a house meant for the guests to rinse their mouth and wash the hands. But in present days these basins have become nothing but ornamental features. The distance of the water-basin from the house and its size are in proportion to the size of the building. A small house may have a basin lm tall, whereas in front of a large house the basin becomes as tall as 2 to 2.5 m and thus making useless as a place of washing, but remains there as an ornamental feature. In such cases, if need be, often a smaller basin is provided near the veranda for practical utility. The basins are generally fitted with an ornamental lid.

The water-basin comes in various shapes, the most common ones are in the shape of an urn. But square-star shaped, cylindrical, stone-bottle shaped, and bowl shaped basins are also quite common. Water basins even resembling the volcanic mountain Fuji are also available. A screen-fence is provided near the water-basin to screen off unwelcome sight. Stones are placed at the base of the water-basin to arrest the splash of water which otherwise may wet the space below the veranda. The sides along these stones are raised either by clay or concrete and a drainage hole is provided which is camouflaged by a number of pebbles. A lantern is provided near by for illumination. Near a tea house the basins are placed low as the persons using these do so in stopping position as per custom.

(i) Stone Lanterns

Stone lantern is an important features of any Japanese garden. The usual stone used is granite, but sand stone or white marble may also be used. The latter one is specially used for "Snow-Scene" type of lantern.

The usual places of fixing the lanterns are near the base of a hill, on an island, on the banks of a lake, near a water-basin or a well, along a path, on a boat-landing, near waterfalls, and a bridge. The lanterns are used singly but along with a combination of rocks, fences, water-basins, shrubs and trees.

The lanterns are not exactly meant for illumination but as objects of ornaments. Even when a lantern is lit in the night, the light emitted hardly illuminates the place because mostly a group of bushes are grown near it. The object of illumination then becomes a dim mysterious glow. When a lantern is near a river bank, this is lit to have red reflection on the water surface.

A lantern has six parts, namely, the ornamental top, cap, light chamber, middle stand, post, and base. These may be of various sizes and shapes. The size should be in proportion to the building or the other garden features around the lantern. The first lantern was erected in Japan in the seventh century by the son of Emperor Suiko.

Lanterns looking of age are valued much and may people make the lanterns look old by artificial means. One such method is to attach moss to the lantern.

(j) Stones

These stones are selected according to size, shape, and colour. No stone should be disproportionate to the size of the garden or the features around it, like a lantern or a water basin. The stones are rarely placed in isolation but rather arranged in groups of two to five. Each group will have stones of various heights and shapes. All stones must be arranged with a firm foundation as stones of unstable nature show the weakness of a garden design. The principle governing the arrangement of stones is to make them look natural. For this purpose, low-growing bushes or upright trees are planted near the stone groupings depending upon the size of the nearby stones.

Naturally, the size, shape, and colour of the stones vary according to the purpose and the place of their use. Accordingly, the stones on a hill, on the blanks of lakes or streams, and near water cascades vary in their shape, size, and ornamental features.

(k) Pagodas

Another favourite feature of Japanese landscape is the stone tower or the pagoda which is a structure consisting of two, three, five, or more separately roofed stages.

(l) Fences and Gates

Fences in a Japanese garden are of two types, one is for partition, while the other is for the purpose of screening which are called "Sleeve Fences". The latter type is so named as its shape resembles that of the long sleeve of a lady's Kimono.

The partition fences should look light in appearance and hence wood and twigs of bamboo are preferred to stone.

The screen fences are meant for covering something which is not pleasant in sight. This is made of wood or bamboo (whole or split or twigs) woven into patterns thus giving it an artistic look so that it can stand on its own in the garden as a feature of ornamentation.

There are generally two gates, one is the front entrance and second the back entrance. Gates are also made of light materials such as wood or bamboo. Some gates are bare while others are roofed. The roof may be made of bamboo, wood, or simply thatched.

(m) Vegetation

The initial step in a Japanese garden is to decide the contours of land and water. Then comes the arrangement of principal rocks which are of primary importance in a Japanese garden as these forms the basic structure or the skeleton of the garden. After the stones, the secondary garden framework, i.e, the evergreen plants, are arranged. The trees are of permanent nature and stand as reference points in the garden. Time and again it has been told that the aim of a Japanese garden is to imitate nature by using natural elements, and hence, there is hardly any bar in using any plant material which serves this purpose. There is a tendency among the garden enthusiasts to introduce plants of Japanese origin in the Japanese gardens even in India.

The Japanese use both needle-leaved and abroad-leaved trees in their garden. The board principles using the plants in the; proper manner are indicated below:

(*i*) To give a larger perspective to a comparatively small garden, the central area is kept clear of trees and shrubs and plantings are restricted to the sides and corners.

(*ii*) An endeavor should be made to give the garden a distant view by catching natural scenery, say a group of rocks or a grove of bamboos, outside the boundary.

(*iii*) Try to avoid putting all the plants on the same plane. Difference in levels may be created by making a sunken area or a small mound. This breaks monotony.

(*iv*) Plants of right shape and size should be used so that they do not look out of scale to the size of the garden.

(*v*) While planting, proper spacing should be given. Plants should neither be put in large groups which cause overcrowding, nor should they be scattered individually. Small groups of plants related in form and texture but differing in height look better. Such groups are never put in rigid straight lines, but are arranged naturally.

(*vi*) Japanese do not prefer to bring in large varieties of plants in a single garden as this goes against the principle of unit. It is advisable to use only a few varieties. In some Japanese gardens the entire planting may be done with only one species of plant.

(*vii*) It will go against the principle of nature if plants of seaside, forest, or desert are combined together.

(*viii*) The Japanese use flowering plants sparingly in their gardens as too many colours go counter to unity. When flowering plants are used, they are planted in between the evergreens.

(*ix*) It is good practice to use plants which change their leaf colour in the autumn or put forth colourful leaves in the spring. The examples of some such trees and shrubs are: maple, *Cryptomeria japonica, Terminalia catappa, Lagerstroemia flos reginae,* and *Ficus religiosa*. The deciduous trees are never planted in the front garden except in a tea garden, as the bare branches may not look attractive during the winter.

Some typical trees of Japanese gardens are:

(*i*) **Evergreens**: Pines, different species of *Abies, Cryptomeria japonica, Podocarpus macrophylla,* and *Juniperus chinensis;*

(*ii*) **Deciduous**: Maples (Acer species), Poplars (*Populus* sp.) Mulbery, (*Morus alba*), and *Salix babylonica* (willow);

(*iii*) **Flowering:** The most commonly used plants are different Prunus species, besides *Magnolia grandiflora* and others.

The commonly grown shrubs are: *Aucuba japonica, Azaleas, Gardenia florida, Nandina domestica, Camellia, Lagestroemia indica,* and Rhododendrons.

Bamboos play a special role in the Japanese gardens. The striking patterns of shadow cast by the arching bamboos against paved path, fences, and patios look beautiful. A paved path in the entrance garden bordered by bamboos simulates a grove.

The traditional Japanese gardens look chiefly green, devoid of any bold colours of flowers. To cultivate the theme of permanence and restfulness trees and shrubs are more appropriate. But, if at all flowers are to be used, the choice should be limited to a few. While planting flowers, remember not to put long beds or borders of flowers in the main garden. In any specific area only one type of flower in a group should be planned, thus avoiding mixed planting. Traditional Japanese will put only one type of flower in one garden, but a non-traditional enthusiast will be well advised to limit his choice only up to three kinds.

The Flowers

The Japanese use more commonly are: chrysanthemums, asters (*e.g., Aster fastigiatus, A. glehnii, A. microcephalus*), carnation, different lilies, irises, lotuses, peonies, and orchids.

Among the vines, (*Clematis, Lonicera japonica, Ipomoea hederacea* (*Syn. Pharbitis headeacea*), *I. Purpurea* (*Syn. Pharbitis purpurea*) *Trachelosermum jasminoides,* and *Wisteria sinensis* are often used.

Chapter 13

Layout of Formal Gardens

Formal garden is laid out in a symmetrical and geometrical pattern and characteristic features are design is stiff. The land is made to fit the plan. All designs are done in straight and narrow way. Formal garden is generally introvert. Flower beds, borders and shrubbery are arranged in geometrically designed beds. Trimmed formal hedges, Cypress, Ashoka trees and topiary are typical features of a formal garden. The world famous Italian, Mughal, Persian and French gardens are regarded as formal gardens for their stiff deigns.

Italian Gardens

The Italian garden style came into existence at the time of Renaissance (14-16 century *BC*). The Italian gardens were influenced by the Persian garden style *i.e.* use of heavy masonry features. The Italian Renaissance and Baroque gardens created during the period of 16th ^{and} 17th centuries were formal and unrelated to nature.

In these styles of gardening the use of heavy masonry features, through the character of masonry was different in the Italian style. The Italian elites conceived their gardens just as an extension of the lavish palaces, as a glamorous outdoor hall for entertainment and for showing off their wealth as well as status.

Italian gardens were formal romantic gardens which were dominated by architectural features. Flower beds and hedges formed an integral part of the architecture. The gardens that enclosed the *villas* and palaces of noble and rich people located on hill slopes were developed to display their wealth.

They conceived their gardens just as an extension of their lavish palaces, as a glamorous outdoor hall for entertainment. With the fall of the Roman Empire the art of gardening sharply declined in Italy. The greatest benefit the Italian garden style brought to gardening is that it taught the entire Europe that gardening could be a most respectable form of art which demands thorough and careful study.

Important Features

The important features include Fountains, Sculptures, Water canals, Hedges, Edges of box or yew plants, Topiary, Arbour, Trellis, Architecturally beautiful buildings, Stairs of marble, Decorative urns and Cypress trees and roses.

Some of the important gardens in Italy are: Villa d'Este Gardens at Tivoli, Villa Carlotta, Como, Medici Villas near Florence, Boboli Gardens, Florence, Villa Balbianello, Lenno, Villa Taranto, Lake Maggiore, Giardino Giusti, Verona, Parco Giardino Sigurtà, Frascati Villas near Rome and La Mortella, Ischia.

French Gardens

Before, 16th century France, the court life was shrouded with stiff formality and exactness. Matching with that the French style of garden designs were also very intricate and artificial. Until this time the French gardens were nothing but copies of Italian style. The new style of gardening now known as French style is largely, rather solely, due to the efforts of **Le Notre** who served in the Royal Garden of Louis XIV from 1643 to 1700. He elevated the art of garden design to a standard which had never since been reached. It was Le Notre who showed to the world the impact in impressiveness of scale, on garden design. His main creations, the gardens at Versailles, have avenues which are memorable for their tremendous length and width. To design a garden at Vauxe-le-Vicomte, his first master piece, Le Notre had removed three villages to create his vista. **The moral of French garden style of Le Notre seems to teach the lesson "How to Think Big".** The style of Le Notre can be termed as an evolution and mastery of the art of formal garden in its perfection. His style dominated the gardens of civilized Europe, for a long time.

Features of French Gardens

(*i*) Characterised by a system of route through the woods linking goodlooking features leading to different vistas.

(*ii*) Gardens give an effect of spaciousness and simplicity.

(*iii*) Appears closely related to nature.

(*iv*) Implementation of scale on garden design.

(*v*) Gardens with tremendous length and width.

Some of the important gardens of Italy are: The Gardens of Versailles, Monet's Garden, Château de Villandry, Jardin des Tuileries and Bagatelle Gardens.

Persian Gardens

These gardens are one of the oldest. The Persian garden style and the Japanese style both were based on their respective ideas of heaven. Except this similarity the two styles differ widely from one another. The Persian styles wee strictly formal and symmetrical. They used for their gardens all crafted materials such as masonry, carved and pierced marble stones, and highly polished stones. The Persian gardens were laid out by cutting terraces on the hill slopes. They also tapped some natural spring to create a straight water-course through the gardens and manipulated the water-course to undertake different movements along its run. If there was no natural source of water this was created artificially by diverting some rivulet or a stream. So the main stay of a Persian garden design was *nahars* (flowing canals) of water – the concept of Persian Paradise, "where cooling water flows". The selection and placing of trees were very judicious. The fruit trees represented the symbol of life while Cypress symbolized death and eternity.

Earlier there were two types of Persian gardens.

1. Royal hunting garden: In this garden, huge acreage of forest land was set aside for the royalty of hunting and horse riding
2. Paradise garden: The Persians used two natural elements viz., water the source of life and the tree whose height was closer to heaven. The theme they followed was from Mesapatomian mythology that there were four rivers of life that divided the land into smaller gardens.

Features of Persian Gardens

1. All crafted materials, such as masonary, carved and pierced marble stones, highly polished stones are used inthese gardens.
2. The gardens are laid by cutting terraces on hill slopes.
3. Water course through the gardens is manipulated to undertake different movements along its run.
4. Main feature of Persian gardens is flowing canals (*nahars*) of water – the concept of Persian paradise, "where cooling water flows".
5. Fruit trees represents the symbol of life while, Cypress symbolises death and eternity.

The notable world famous Persian gardens are: Pasargad Persian Garden at Pasargadae, Iran, Chehel Sotoun, Isfahan, Iran, Fin Garden, Kashan, Iran, Eram Garden, Shiraz, Iran, Shazdeh Garden, Mahan, Kerman, Iran, Dolatabad Garden, Yazd, Iran, Abbasabad Garden, Abbasabad, Mazandaran, Iran, Akbarieh Garden and South Khorasan Province, Iran.

Mughal Gardens

The gardens laid out during the rule of Mughal Emperors in India are known as Mughal gardens. The Mughal gardens are similar to the style of gardens of Central

Asia and Persia. Babar (1494 – 1531) was the first Mughal ruler to introduce this style in India. All other Mughal rulers and some of the Mughal Begums laid their hand on developing one or the other Mughal gardens in India.

Mr. Umar Sheikh Mirza alias Babar was the first person to lay the foundation of the Mughal empire in India in 1526 AD. He laid out a garden at Agra now known as Rambagh.

Akbar (1556 – 1605 AD) built a garden Nasim Bagh close to Dal Lake in Kashmir.

Jahangir (1605-1625 AD) developed gardens at Shalimar, Achhabal and Verinag in Kashmir.

Shah Jahan (1627-1658 AD) established gardens at Red fort and Taj Mahal in Agra in memory of his wife Mumtaz.

Sher Shah Suri (1540-1544 AD) constructed the famous grand trunk road with avenue trees on both sides. Aurangazeb also played a major role in developing gardens in India.

Certain Mughal gardens are there in India which were constructed by various Mughal emperors. Babur built Ram Bagh and Zohra Bagh at Agra, Bagh-I-Wafa and Bagh-I-Kalan at Kabul. The gardens at Fatehpur Sikri and Sikandra at Agra and Nasimbagh at Kashmir were built by Akbar. Shalimar, Achhabal baghs in Kashmir, Dilkhus bagh at Lahore and garden around the tomb of Itmaduddaulal at Agra, were built by Jahangir. Nishat-Bagh in Kashmir was built by Asaf Khan and Pinjore garden was built by Fadaikhan. Shalimar bagh in Lahore and Delhi and Taj garden in Agra were built by Shah Jahan. Mir Alam-bagh at Hyderabad was built by Nawab Salar Jung.

The main features of Mughal gardens, which are largely borrowed from the Persian style, are: (a) site and style of the design, (b) walls, (c) gates, (d) terrace, (e) nahars or running waters, (f) baradari, (g) often a tomb or a mosque, and (h) trees.

Choice of Site

Mughals were very choosy about the selection of site and always preferred a site on a hill slope with a perennial rivulet or along the bank of a river. **Design**: Mughal gardens are generally rectangular or square in shape and different architectural features are the main stay of the design.

Walls and Gates

The Mughals created the gardens not only for pleasure and recreation but also as forts and residences surrounded by high walls and with-an-imposing wooden gate at the entrance which was studded with bold iron nails and pointed iron spikes. **The purpose of the high walls was security from the enemies and shelter against hot winds**. The gardens were a place of peace for the Emperors to enjoy with their wives and concubines.

Terrace

the Mughals came from the hilly terrains and so they were fond of terraces in the gardens. For this reason they used to select the location of gardens near hill slopes. Their fascination for terrace was so intense that even in the plains of Punjab they created artificial terraces.

According to Islamic faith the Paradise has eight divisions and hence some times the gardens have eight terraces corresponding to the eight divisions or occasionally the gardens may be composed of seven terraces also representing the seven planets.

Nahars (Running Water)

The style for having running water by constructing canals and tanks borrowed from the Persians. The water canals were paved with tiles (or marble) of blue colour to create the illusion of depth. The course of water used to be manoeuvred in various ways taking advantage of each slope, however small it may be, to break up the flow into artificial falls and ripples. The water canals used to have fountains to throw up the water high in the air. In the evenings small lamps used to be illuminated to create beautiful reflexions.

The fascination for water came from the Muslim faith which says that the promised paradise is the place "where cooling waters flow". With this bias for water Mughals selected sites on hill slopes to tap a running rivulet or spring for source of water. In the plains of India, where the summers are hot, Mughals utilized water for its cooling effect.

Baradari

This is noting but an arbour-like structure, but made of stone and masonry with a pucca roof and a raised platform for sitting. These were usually provided with twelve or occasionally more doors on all sides for the Emperors to watch the performance of the dancing girls.

Tomb or Mosque

It was a common practice to have the gardens built around a tomb (*e.g.*, Taj Mahal, Akbhar's Tomb at Sikandra). It is often said that the Mughal gardens were at their best when built around a monument.

Plants

(*i*) Trees and Flowers

For the Mughals each tree symbolises something like youth, life, death *etc.* Fruit trees are considered symbols of life and youth. Cypress represents death and eternity.

(*ii*) Flower Beds

Flower beds are constructed near the main building or along the water channels and paths. Usually the permanently built flower beds are of geometrical shape.

Plants Grown in Mughal Gardens

In Kashmir plants planted were, Chinar (*Platanus orientalis*), White poplar (*Poplar alba*), Cypress, apple, peach, plum, cherries (sour and sweet), quince, pomegranate with fig plants

In plains of India plants planted were mango, grape, figs, guava, aonla, orange, citrus, peach, plum *etc.*

They planted Spring flowering trees such as safed kachnar (*Bauhinia alba*), palas (*Butea monosperma*), champa (*Michelia champaka*), chalta (*Dillenia indica*), chandan (*Santalum album*).

Fragrant shrubs like Harshingar (*Nyctanthes arbortristis*), hari champa (*Artabotris odoratissima*), roses, Screw pine, *Jasminum sambac, J. multiflorum, J. grandiflorum,* garhal (*Hibiscus rosasinensis*) and annual flowering plants mainly, narcissus, daffodils, irises, carnations, hollyhock, French marigold, larkspur, stock, ornamental sunflower, amaranthus, cock's comb.

The famous Mughal gardens in the world are: The Shalimar Gardens in Lahore, Pakistan, Mughal gardens at the Taj Mahal, Agra, Shalimar Bagh, Srinagar, Kashmir, Pinjore Gardens in Haryana and Rastrapathi Bhavan, New Delhi.

Chapter 14

Layout of Shade Garden, Sunken and Vertical Gardens

Gardening in shade can be a difficult endeavor without the proper selection of plants. While gardening under the shade of trees, the tree roots compete with the plants grown there for food and water. Planning a shade garden begins with choosing suitable shade garden plants and an understanding of the various types of shade and soil within these areas. By learning more about these factors and plants for shade gardens, you can turn any shady spot into a beautiful garden. No more dealing with dark, dreary landscapes.

The soil under the trees is to be dug deeply to about 25-30cm to cut the surface feeding roots. This operation should be repeated every year by digging deep along the borders of the beds. The plants are to be watered and fertilized separately. The shade garden plants under trees are spaced wider than the open. A shaded place in between two buildings can be developed into a wild garden with a winding path.

Different plants require different degrees of shade ranging from dense shade to dappled or partial shade. The common plants suggested for shade gardens are:

- Heuchera (Coral bells)
- *Lamium maculatum* (Dead nettle).
- *Tiarella cordifolia* (Foamflower).

- ✰ Pulmonaria (Lungwort).
- ✰ Astilbe.
- ✰ Digitalis (Foxglove).
- ✰ Hakonechloa
- ✰ Primula (Primrose).
- ✰ Euphorbia (Spurge).
- ✰ Alchemilla (Lady's mantle).

Sunken Garden

It is laid below the ground level. An existing ditch or a dried out pond may be utilized for laying out a sunken garden or a portion of a garden may be dug to layout such a garden. A provision should be made for proper drainage. The surface runoff water should not fall into the sunken garden. A formal or an informal garden can be laid out in a large sunken garden. The ideal depth of a sunken garden is about 120 cm. The approach to a sunken garden is generally by a staircase preferably made of stones. The surface of the sunken garden can be decorated with crazy paving, gravel path *etc.*

Construction

1. Sunken garden can be laid out in an already existing depression of land or a portion of the garden may be specially dug to lay out such a garden. The ideal depth of a sunken garden is about 120 cm.
2. If sufficient depth is available one or all the walls of the sunken, garden can be developed into dry wall and this will help to support the raised sides of the sunken garden in addition to beauty.
3. Adequate drainage arrangement should be made by putting one or two drainage outlets and connected them to the sewage system.
4. If the garden is likely to be flooded rapidly, special arrangements may have to be made to drain out excess of water accumulated.
5. Some drainage materials such as stones, rubbles *etc.*, may be placed below the surface of the sunken garden at a depth of about 1 m from surface. The thickness may be of 60 cm.
6. In dry areas, to increase humidity in the garden fountains, stream can be added.
7. It is always advisable to have an attractive central feature such as sundial or bird bath or stone figure. This helps tie the composition of garden together.
8. The surface of the sunken garden can be decorated with crazy paving and steps with beds and borders.

Cautions

1. Proper drainage facilities should be provided as the sunken garden is likely to collect water.
2. Sunken garden should not be made in a very heavy soil due to drainage problems.
3. Steps should be taken to prevent the surface runoff water to fall in the sunken garden.

Planting

There is no hard and fast rule as what is to be planted in a sunken garden. This will mainly depend on the area available and the choice of the grower.

While planning the garden, it should be taken into account the portions receiving or not receiving the morning sun and portion under complete shade.

A sunken garden is likely to be more humid, especially in high rainfall areas, than the portions above the ground. Hence, it is likely that moisture loving plants such as ferns, *Ixora,* gardenia *etc.* will do better in such gardens.

Eg: Sunken garden in the Byrant Park, Kodaikanal (Tamil Nadu).

Terrace Garden

A terrace is a raised space of ground constructed around a dwelling house or at the corner of a garden or on the sides of a hill. When this terrace is used for some sort of gardening this is known as terrace gardening. A terrace garden is generally constructed just in front of the house from where a view of the whole garden can be obtained

Construction

A terrace garden is very often referred to as the outdoor living or drawing room and to make it more cozy and private, some sort of walls are to be constructed on the sides.

- ☆ First a low brick or stone retaining wall may be built to handle the change of levels while on the top of it about 90-120 cm tall wall of lace patterned concrete blocks may be built which will provide privacy but will not stop breeze or obstruct light.
- ☆ Wide broad wooden fences can also be used but this will obstruct light and air. Since a terrace is used as an outdoor living room for relaxing, the area should always be nearly dry under the foot. For this particular reason, most people favour a paved terrace.
- ☆ To facilitate easy maintenance, for more comfort as a sitting place and to keep the place dry, paving is done with local stones, flag stones, brick, concrete, wood, gravel and mosaic tiles.

To make a paving, first a hard foundation is made and over that the paving is constructed. Gravel paving is cheapest but has some drawbacks.

Well burnt bricks should be used in an artistic pattern as they are durable. Wood pavings are generally available in the form of rectangular blocks, round sections cut from logs. But these are suitable in mild climate as extreme climate may cause degradation of wood. Wood can be treated with cuprinol, naptox *etc.* to prevent rotting

Planting

After proper planning, planting should be done. First, it is to be decided if the whole area will be paved or some portion will be left out for lawns, beds, *etc.*,. Planting of one or two specimen trees and creepers for training over the house walls can be done.

In general, the parallel surface itself should have very little plant growth. Wide joints of the pavings allow more growth of grass which is difficult to clip and requires more time in maintenance than narrow unplanted joints. Moreover, such joints are hazardous for the ankles of the playing children as well as adults. Too many creeping plants in the joints restrict the movement and reduce the sitting space which is the primary necessity in a terrace garden. Only a few low growing creeping plants such as *Portulaca, Lantana sellowiana* for the tropics and *Thymus serpyllum* and *Veronica repens* for the temperate regions can be recommended for planting in the wider joints. Some small specimen dwarf trees or shrubs can be planted in the middle grass circular, rectangular or square beds left out. But such plants should fit with the architectural design of the house and should also be most ornamental with an interesting look. Potted plants also can be kept. In no case plants should obstruct vision and screen the architecture of the house.

Various garden features like hanging baskets, lilypool, sundial or bird bath, sculpture can be placed in a suitable corner. Sitting arrangement can be made for resting and comfort.

E.g., Terrace garden in the Byrant Park Kodaikanal (Tamil Nadu), Llyod Botanical garden, Darjeeling (West Bengal).

Chapter 15

Layout of Rock Garden and Gravel Garden

An ornamental planting in rocky places or in areas on which rocks have been placed for the particular purpose to make congenial conditions for certain classes of plants and also to lend interest and variety to a part of garden is called rockery or rock garden. The desire to cherish the natural mountainous range, has brought to exist the concept of rock gardening. Rock garden breaks the monotony of a level garden. Its purpose is not to have a geological collection or display but rather a place to grow rock plants. Rock gardens are originally developed in an effort to plant and beautify natural rocky places or possibly an accumulation of rocks left by a stream. A rock garden should be built only if it fits in with the general design of the garden. Another purpose is to grow alpine plants that various gardeners had seen during their travels in mountainous regions.

Rocks and soils are arranged such a fashion that conditions is created for the growth of different plants.

In nature, rocks may be getting covered with different colored moss and if soil collected in cracks and crevices of rocks, plants grow there naturally.

Selection of Site

It is easy to create rock garden where natural rocks are available nearby. But large rock garden should be situated in a place where there will fit with the other garden features. Apart from this corners, middle part of informal garden, under large trees are better places for creating rock garden.

Characteristics of Rocks

The rocks should be of local origin, porous and have a weathered look. Stones having diameter of **60cm** or more should be selected.

Types of Rock Gardens

1. Naturalistic Rock Garden

Naturalistic rock gardens are best used on a natural slope. The rock used should be well weathered, and of local origin. In a natural slope the lower should be the rock garden. In fact the garden itself should not be more than a foot or at most 60 cm. The rock should be placed in natural horizontal positions rather than vertically or at angles. Rock should be half buried to give the appearance of age and permanence. Soft dolomite limestones with holes and pockets weathered in them give an opportunity for planting. Extremely porous rock like tufa usually appears artificial. Only one kind of rock should be used in any one garden.

For permanence, appearance and ease of upkeep, no rocks of 10 kg or less than 30 cm in diameter should be used. For small garden 10-50 kg rocks are used, where as for large garden it may vary up to 1-2 tonne, or several smaller rocks may be grouped together to give the effect of large one.

2. Moraine Garden

A moraine garden is a type of rock garden with or without rocks, in which a gritty, well drained soil mixture is under laid by water a foot or so beneath the surface. The purpose of the water flow in the rock garden is a constant supply of moisture to the roots of the plants. This is to duplicate the conditions under which many alpine plants are found growing in nature, where the water from melting snows flows beneath the rock surface.

For complete drainage, the soil in the moraine should consist of equal parts of loam, leaf mould, sand and stone chips with a layer of ½ inch of stone chips on the surface.

3. Seree Garden

It is similar to moraine garden except the inclusion of water beneath the surface.

4. Alpine Meadow or Alpine Lawn Garden

Modification of naturalistic rock garden. More or less spreading alpines are planted thickly in a gentle slope or open flat areas. It is with or without occasional rocks.

5. Wall Garden

The wall garden is the most practicable form of rock garden, the type best adapted to the average yard. For this a wall is made without cement which is called aury wall. The site of the wall can be kept 30-150 cm high and 1-1.5m long but it should be in rectangular shape and according to the yards in the house. If it is to be made more than 1m high, the layers will be started from beneath the ground.

a. Tyre type of rockery
b. Round rockery
c. Rectangular rockery
d. Square rockery
e. Rockery under tree
f. Alpine rockery
g. Flat type rockery

Construction Procedure

1. First plan of the rock garden should be prepared on paper.
2. Selected site should be marked out by using bars and pegs.
3. The base should be filled with sufficient quantity of broken bricks small stones and sand for proper drainage.
4. Form the mound of required height by filling sufficient quantity of soil, the mound should be allowed to settle for some time and formed by beating.
5. Create the steps, place the stones on the mound, the stone should be placed in a slightly slanting position gently leaning backwards, so that rain water and during watering, it flows towards the plant roots.
6. Sufficient number of pockets is created between stones for growing plants. While placing rocks side by side, they should be placed as close as possible otherwise soil will be washed away. Gaps between two stones should be covered with **concrete**. Concrete should be restricted to minimum.
7. Add garden soils up to a depth of 30 cm. Mix together equal parts of sand and farmyard manure.
8. Position the plants along with the pots so that you can see how they look and can move them around easily, if necessary.
9. Use a trowel to take out a hole a little larger than root ball, plant is at correct depth, then tight loose soil around the roots and firms it well.
10. Finish off rockery by covering the surface by small pebbles, which increases the beauty and prevents soil erosion.

Maintenance

Weeding

Periodical weeding is necessary to remove the weeds, which are competing with plants. Besides all dried and dead leaves should be removed from the branches of the plants.

Stalking

Stalking is necessary for newly planted tall plants to prevent the physical damages and to obtain the straight growth.

Watering

Regular watering is necessary to keep the plants healthy and attractive. Watering should be done at least once in three days. Drip system of irrigation may also be adopted.

Replacement of Soil

Rockery plants need replacing of soil at least every 2-3 years as the soil become sour and infertile.

Manuring

Plants may be top dressed every year with compost consisting of a good garden soil, sand and fine leaf mould in equal proportion to the top few centimeters of soil is scraped out and in its place new compost is filled in along with a little quantity (125 g) bone meal depending upon the plants. Periodically rock plants should be fed with liquid manure also.

Suitable Plants

Annuals

All annuals may be accommodated in the rockery depending on their height in between shrubs and other perennial plants. For instance Asclepias, Calliandra, Clerodendron, Crossandra, Cuphea, Euphorbia. Zinnia, Phlox, Verbena.

Shrubs

Duranta, Juniferous, Lantana sellowiana, Russelia juntia, Thuja orientalis etc.

Cacti and Succulents

Adiantum, Pony tail plant, Opentia, Cerus, Mumalaria, Agave, Kalanchoe, Sansiveria, Yacca, Hawarthia, Furcrea, Sedum etc.

Ferns

Nephrolepsis, Polypodium and Adiantum **etc.**

Shade Plants

Imparatiens sultaniana, Pedilanthes tithymaloides, Pilea muscosa, Portulaca sps, minature roses, Zebrana pendula, Tradescantia albifolia, Vincea rosea etc.

Besides to above plants, with careful selection of large group of annuals, bulbous plants, other shrubs and other ornamental plants can be selected and grown in the rockery depending upon the necessity and environmental condition.

After care

Proper training and pruning should be done to prevent overcrowding. Regulation of watering and nutrition should be done according to the plant species.

Some famous rock gardens in India are Lalbagh, Bengaluru (Karnataka); Sim's Park Coonoor (Tamil Nadu) and The Agri Horticultural Society Garden, Kolkata (West Bengal).

Gravel Gardens

Gravel is an inexpensive and flexible alternative to paving of a lawn. It can be used in both formal and informal designs.

Types of Gravels

Gravels comes in different sizes and colors. Some types are angular, others are rounded, some are white, and others are assorted shades of green or red.

Gravel Path

It is often used as drives, but it is also good choice for informal paths with in the garden. However it is not a good choice for paths where you will have to wheel the mower.

How to Lay a Gravel Path?

a. Excavate the area to a depth of 15 cm and ram the base firm
b. Provide brick or stout edge to retain the gravel
c. First place a layer of compacted hardcore. Add a mixture of sand and course gravel.
d. Top up to the required height with the final grade gravel. Rake and roll the gravel repeatedly until the surface is firm and stable.

Gravel Beds

Gravel can be used as straight substitute for grass and require much less maintenance.

How to Lay a Gravel Bed?

a. Excavate the area to required depth of about 15 cm.
b. Level the ground lay heavy duty black polythene or a mulching sheet over the area.
c. Then spread the gravel on top and rake level.
d. To plant through the gravel, draw it back from the planting area and make a slit in the polythene plant normally.

Firm in and pull back the polythene before recovering with gravel.

Chapter 16

Layout of Roof Gardens

There is a misconception in India between roof gardening and terrace gardening. In many articles the gardening on the roof is often termed as terrace gardening which is not strictly correct according to British practice. Terrace gardening is completely different from roof gardening.

The fundamental difference between ground gardening and roof gardening is that, at ground level the depth may be unlimited with source of groundwater. Whereas on roof the depth of the soil is shallow not exceeding 30-45 cm. Not only depth is shallow in roof garden, but also the drainage is also good and hence water has to be replenished constantly by frequent watering. Large trees and plants are generally not grown on the roof as the roof below limits the growth of the taproot. Container plants may be kept on verges or bricks. Over the roof adequate drainage should be provided for the rain and excess irrigation water to drain off quickly. Water garden, rock garden, lawn, hanging baskets, climbers may form of part of roof garden. Always allow for the vertical growth rather than horizontal growth.

In modern times, homes with a compound and lawn especially in cities and towns are becoming rare replacing such homes. As a result, the private home gardens are vanishing and the only places left for gardening are the roofs of houses and the balcony. A spacious and well-planned roof garden can be a place of joy and recreation. In bigger cities of India, many of the large hotels and public buildings are developing this type of gardening. Even in Lucknow a hotel has a roof garden with lawn, though needs proper planning. Many private houses in Delhi, Kolkata, Mumbai, and Baroda have roof gardens, including a lawn. The roof garden of Dr B P Pal in Delhi, dominated by a collection of roses, besides other plants such as bougainvillea, pansy, *etc.*, is a charm by its own right. There are many other private homes in our cities having charming roof gardens with rare collections of cacti, orchids, dahlia, chrysanthemum, and other plants.

Advantages of Roof Garden

1. Since the roof of an open atmosphere air and sunlight available in plenty. Therefore, plants grow healthy in such environment.
2. High elevation minimizes the attack of pests and diseases.
3. Roof garden is out of bound for pilferage and damage by animals.
4. The beauty of garden can be enjoyed from close range during day and night.
5. The therapeutic value of gardening on physical and mental health can be utilized to its fullest advantage in such gardening.

Disadvantages

1. Quantity of growing media is much less here therefore supply of moisture and nutrients to the plants are limited.
2. Shallow depth of the soil results in poor root anchorage subjecting the plants to lodging on the open roof.

With the increased problems of space in cities and towns for growing plants, the importance of roof gardening cannot be ignored. Though there are limitations, by applying imagination and visualization an attractive garden can be made on roof top.

Types of Roof Gardens

Roof top gardens may be private or co-operative in nature. When the garden is constructed on a private building, usually under single ownership, it is private in nature.

In the multistoried buildings many owners will be there and if a garden is established on the roof of such buildings, its ownership will be considered co-operative in nature.

Suitability of the Roof

The strength of the roof to bear the weight of soil is the first consideration before making to start. This has to be taken care while constructing a building.

Drainage is the most important aspect as it may pose a problem to the roof. Therefore, roof should be made water proof/leak proof to avoid the drainage caused to the roofs.

Spreading of asphalted canvas or thick polythene sheet may serve the purpose of water proofing for a few seasons. When the construction of the roof has been made with perfect load bearing the whole roof can be utilized for developing the garden, or in other cases, a strip of land 60 to 70 cm wide along the side of the load bearing wall may be chosen for planting.

Limitations: The difficulties encountered in a roof garden are completely different from that of gardens at the ground level. Since the garden is at a high level from the ground, the cost maintenance may go up as everything has to be carried up. But the more fundamental difference is in the depth of the soil. At ground level the depth may be unlimited with a source of groundwater, whereas on the roof the depth of the soil is shallow, not exceeding 90 cm, but generally varying between 20 and 60 cm. Not only the depth is shallow in roof garden, but the drainage is also good and hence water has to be replenished constantly by frequent watering. Large trees and shrubs are generally not grown on the roof as the growth of the tap root is limited by the roof below. Moreover, because of shallow depth, good drainage and frequent watering, the plant food in the soil leaches off more rapidly and is to be made good by more frequent replacement.

Planning

Before planning a roof garden certain points are to be checked. Flower beds can be made directly on the roof. This can be achieved by placing the soil between the outer wall or the parapet and a wall built on the inner side with the help of moisture-proof wood shuttering stones, or bricks. The width of such boxes will vary according to the available space, the nature of the plants to be grown, and other factors. Such beds directly constructed on the roof surface are not preferred always, as they are of permanent nature and may also damage the roof. Alternatively, the best method will be to arrange a series of containers holding soil, such as boxes, pots troughs, tubs, *etc.*, These are placed over wedges or bricks to leave a clear gap between them and the roof for proper drainage and passage of air.

The first thing to check before starting a roof garden is whether the roof surface can bear the weight of the soil. Soil, especially wet soil, is much heavier than one can usually conceive. Secondly, the roof should be made water-proof to prevent seepage of water into the room below and finally, it should have adequate drainage so that rain and irrigation water drains off quickly.

The concept of roof gardening itself is artificial; therefore, while planning and designing this point should be kept in mind. As for example, it is not possible to create natural scenery with hills and valleys or natural forest scenery. As for any other gardening a roof garden should also have a dominant focal point, like lawn or water garden or rock garden or a prominent climber (*e.g.*, *Bougainvillea*, *Clerodendron splendens*, *Bignonia venusta*, climbing rose).

On a roof the space available for gardening is limited; therefore, it will be a good idea to encourage vertical growth. This is the reason why a roof garden lover should use **more climbers** and trailers in his garden, some of which can climb over a supporting pillar while others can grow rampantly over the boundary wall and spill over the top and hang down the side of the building. *Ficus repens* is a good root climber which can cover a wall. Other attractive creepers include *Cobaea scandens* (annual), railway creeper, *Vernonia elaegnifolia*, passion flower, *Thunbergia alata* (annual), *etc.*

The Media

The media should be prepared by mixing equal parts of garden soil and cow dung manure or leaf mould. Layout of the garden should be marked on the roof with powdered lime. The media should be spread 15-20 cm thick leaving the paths lines with bricks. A gap of 5 mm between two bricks should be held at every 50 cm length to act as a drainage hole. A close knit nylon screen along the inner side of the brick lining prevents soil drainage. One kg of oilcake of neem or *karanja* seeds, one kg of bonemeal, small charcoal bits should be worked in every 10 m^2 of newly prepared beds. pH of media/soil to be maintained at 6.2 to 6.8.

Loam free, light weight potting composts and plastic or fiberglass containers are used rather than terracotta or cement pots. Everything possible to keep down the weight should be done.

Hose pipe to connect to a tap indoors is also cumbersome. So we should give preference for installing an automatic watering system.

Maintenance

Due to limited quantity of soil in the roof garden, plants should be watered quite frequently. A number of troughs can be placed in the garden for water supply. To reduce the cost of watering, pipelines with spray nozzles may be laid overhead and connected to a tap with high water pressure.

1. The practices such as staking and pruning may be followed timely
2. Nutrition may be given judiciously
3. Neem oil and soap emulsion or decoction may be used as insecticides for plant protection

Selection of Planting Material

Plants of small to medium stature giving mass flowering and attractive foliage over a long period of the year should be chosen for a roof garden. Hardy and drought tolerant ornamentals would also do well. The plants to be chosen are:

Annuals

For summer: Amaranthus, balsam, celosia, coleus, coreopsis, gaillardia, globe amaranth, portulaca, torenia, zinnia, kochia

For winter: Ageratum, alyssum, antirrhinum, aster, brachycome, annual chrysanthemum, cornflower, clarkia, cosmos, annual carnation, poppy, candytuft, daisy, dahlia, gypsophilla, hollyhock, larkspur, linaria, linium, lupin, marigold, salvia, sweet pea, sweet sultan, sweet William, verbena, zinnia.

Bulbous Plants

Cannas, caladium, gladiolus, football lily, belladonna lily, amaryllis.

Shrubs

Small and medium shrubs like acalypha, beloperone, yesterday – today –

tomorrow, clerodendron, eranthemum, graptophylum, jasmine, *Russelia juncea, Thunbergia erecta,* bougainvillea, bottle brush. The growth of these plants can be restricted by growing in pots.

Climbers

Glory lily, morning lily, sweet pea, *Jasminum auriculatum* can be placed along the posts and pillars or on arches on the roof.

Trees

Araucaria sp., *Bix ovellana, Ficus* sp., *Salix babylonica, Pinus longifolia, Thevetia peruviana* can be kept dwarf by growing in pots and used in the roof garden.

Roses

Any garden is incomplete without roses. A good bed for roses can be prepared by constructing 8 cm thick and 40 cm high brick wall besides the one of the boundary of the roof garden.

Chapter 17

Layout of Paved Garden

Paved garden is one of the attractive features of a garden. There are some specific plants, which adapt themselves well to a paved garden. These should be dwarf in nature and stand a considerable amount of wear and tear from shoes of different weights. But a paved garden should be laid in a path, which is not used very often. A special paved garden may also be created, if a path suitable for this is not available. Ordinarily a paved garden is meant for walking, although not very frequently and hence the interstices of the paved garden should be planted sparingly.

The foundation of the paved garden should be prepared in the same manner as for an ordinary pathway. Proper drainage should be ensured for the paved garden plants. After the foundation is laid, a good soil, preferably of lighter texture, is laid to depth of about 10 cm. Before laying the stones over this, 2-3 weeks' time should be given to the soils to settle. The stones selected should not be less than 25-cm in dia; otherwise the paved garden looks clumsy. For paths, rectangular stones are more suitable, whereas for circles and squares irregular stones of any shape or size can be used. Between two stones gaps of about 4-8 cm are left and the stones are laid in an informal pattern. These spaces are filled with good soil and traces of bone meal are also added. The bounder of the paved garden is usually supported by any adjoining feature, these should be cemented as in the case of a crazy path. When the sides are supported by stones, the plants grown to cover these are allowed to grow a little inside the paved garden in an informal manner to give a more natural effect.

Planting should be done with discretion and over-planting should be avoided. The crevices should not be filled completely, rather the plants should be placed irregularly either in small group or in isolated patches. A dense planting will look unnatural and will have very little appeal. In a sparsely planted paved garden even the worst clumsy visitor will be able to avoid tramping of a plant in flower.

Choosing the Right Paving Materials

- ☆ **Sandstone:** Widely available, Huge color range and Easy to work with
- ☆ **Gravel:** Inexpensive, Attractive texture and Easy to install
- ☆ **Slate:** Attractive and Easy to shape
- ☆ **Granite:** Durable and Huge color range
- ☆ **Limestone:** Evenly colored and Easy to shape

Some of the good ideas for layout of paved gardens are:

1. Repurpose some street stones.
2. Mix dull tones with color
3. Play with pattern.
4. Add modern steppingstones.
5. Go freestyle.
6. Go traditional.
7. Get setts.
8. Use the same stone in different ways
9. Step up (or down).
10. Work in special details.
11. Be stylish on a budget.

Some of the plants suitable for a paved garden are listed below:

- ☆ *Achillea rupestris* (Compositae): A mat-forming, tufted plant with white –yellow flower heads.
- ☆ *A. tomentosa* (Compositae): A compact, mat-forming plant with bright-yellow flower heads.
- ☆ *Alyssum montanum* (Cruciferae): A dwarf (7-8 cm), prostrate, tufted plant which bear many-flowered recemes with bright-yellow and fragrant flowers.
- ☆ *Dianthus deltoids* (Caryopyllaceae): Commonly called 'Maiden Pink' is a prostrate dwarf (12-20 cm) herbaceous plant, bearing purples to crimson-red flowers with dark strips and bright spots.
- ☆ *Geranium pylzowianum* (Geraniaceae): A slender, dwarf (30 cm tall) plant bearing purple flowers.
- ☆ *Hymenatherum tenuifolium*: A herbaceous perennial or annual of prostrate habit, the fern-like foliage is finely divided and beautiful. Flowering is round the year.

- *Lantana sellowiana, Gysophila repens,* Porulaca (Perennial type),Setcresea palida and S. purpuria,Verbena erinoides,Vinca rosea: Viola cornuta: Zebrina pendula: *Euphorbia splendens prostrata*:
- *Zinnia linearis*: A gardener should be able to add many more plants by practical experience.

Chapter 18

Layout of Marsh or Bog Garden

Many people have reservations regarding the name 'Bog Garden', as an actual bog is an area where there is stagnant acid water and only plants such as sundew, butter words, *etc.*, grow. But the bog garden which we find in landscape gardening is actually a marsh where the soil is not acidic and a shallow stream or trickle runs through it.

Marsh Garden

In a marsh garden, a shallow stream runs through it. The site of a marsh garden should be low lying where the surface drainage water will collect naturally. A site having a sub-soil of sticky clay is ideally suitable for a marsh garden should never exceed a depth of 60 cm. All parts of the marsh garden is made accessible by laying paths of rough stones or bricks, winding round the marsh and putting stepping stones over them. Plants growing under submerged conditions, flowing conditions and those, which grow above the saturated soil but near the stream, may be selected. A pond is not an essential feature of any bog garden, but, if there is any adjacent pond, the overflow water can be used to keep the marsh garden moist. The main criterion of a marsh garden is to keep it moist and in a swampy state all throughout. For this reason, the site of the marsh garden should be low lying where the surface drainage water will collect naturally. A site having a sub soil of sticky clay is ideally suitable for marsh garden as only a trickle of water will keep this wet. But, if the soil is light in nature, certain amount of digging will be needed before establishing a marsh garden.

Construction

1. The whole area intended to be developed into a marsh garden is dug up to a depth of 60 cm and a thin layer of clay up to 10-12 cm deep is placed at the bottom to form the base of the marsh garden.
2. Then a 12 cm layer of rubble of large stones is placed over this to ensure that the water in the marsh does not become stagnant.
3. The rest of the hollow is filled with a compost of garden loam and leaf mould in the proportion of 1: 1 and the level made up with the surrounding land
4. All parts of the marsh garden are made accessible by laying paths of rough stones or bricks, winding round the marsh and putting steeping stones over them.

Keeping this in view the paths through the marsh garden should be laid at different levels so as to divide the marsh into shelving beds of different heights enabling the plants to find the right type of growing conditions.

Plants

Marsh plants can be categorized into three broad groups:

1. First group: Plants loving 5 to 10 cm of standing water swamp dwellers.
2. Second group: Plants live on or a little above the water line, with their roots standing in water logged soil.
3. Third group: Plants grow above the saturated soil, but near enough to send their roots in search of water.

In small area, it is advisable to create a greater variety by growing the dwarf marsh plants. But in a vast area the vigorous growing ones should be used more freely, especially to create background effects.

Plants Suitable for Marsh Garden

Scientific Name of Plant (English Name)	*Zone*	*Height*	*Character*	*Season of Flowering*
Acorus calamus (Sweet flag)	S	60 cm	The leaves 60-90 cm long, 1-2 cm width	Summer
Alocasia amazonica	M	60 cm	Beautiful broad leaves of sagittate cordate shape	June-August
Arundinaria (Bamboo dwarf)	WM	30 cm to 2.5 m	Leaves bamooo like	All year round
Arundo donax (Giant Reed)	M	3.5 m	Leaves 30-60 cm long, 3-5 cm broad. The varie- gated species have white margin	Autumn
Asplenium (Fern)	MW	10-60 cm	Fronds are of evergreen nature	—do—
Calla palustris (Bog Arum)	SN	15 cm	Leaves shiny, spathe white, flowering arum like	June-July

Scientific Name of Plant (English Name)	Zone	Height	Character	Season of Flowering
Caltha palustris (Double marsh marigold)	MW	25 cm	The showiest caltha with bright yellow double flowers	March-May
Cypripedium spectabile (An orchid)	M	45-90 cm	Flowers white or flushed rose	June
Eriophorum sp. (Cotton grass)	W	45-60 cm	Plumes silky white	Summer
Filipendula palmata	M	60-90 cm	Flowers pink turning white	Summer
Hemerocallis aurantiaca (Day lily)	M	30-60 cm	Leaves narrow, grass like, flowers funnel shaped, in many shades	Summer to Autumn
Hosta glauca (Plantain Lily)	M	60 cm	Bold foliage plants for group planting	Summer
Iris karmpferi	WM	60 cm	—do—	June-July
Lysimachia nummularia (Creeping jenny or charlie money wort	WM	Prostrate flowers	Stem spreading studded with yellow	June-August
Osmunda regalis (Royal Fern)	WM	90-180 cm	A good plant for making clump at borders of water	—do—
Pandanas odoratissimus (Screwpine Keora, Ketaki, keya)	SW	2-15 m	Bears scented flowers to be proved to keep dwarf	Summer
Primula (Candelabra types)	M	30-60 cm	*P. aurantiaca*, flowers orange red, *P. japonica*, crimson, suitable for mild and flowers in temperate climate	May–July
Primula florindae (Giant cowslip)	WM	90 cm	One of the best primulas for a wet place. Suitable for mild temperature climate. Flowers sulphur yellow	July-August

Codes: S: Roots in soil sub-merged by a few cm of water; W: Roots in moist soil, but crown at or not much above water level; M: Crown above saturated soil, but roots within the reach of sufficient moisture.

Cautions

1. A marsh garden should never exceed a depth of 60 cm though its spread will depend upon the available area and choice.
2. It should never suffer from drought and be kept sufficiently moist by a trickle of water at the same time avoiding stagnation.
3. It must be noted that all plants need water but in varying degrees.
4. Overcrowding of plants should be avoided, *e.g.*, Bog garden in Govt. Botanic Gardens, Ootacamund.

Chapter 19

Landscaping of Places of Public Importance

The most important elements in successful public urban green space are plants. People are always astonished to find something natural and beautiful in the middle of a big city. Whether it is an old garden, a community garden, or a spectacular urban flower display, people simply feel better about themselves and their communities when surrounded by beautiful plants. Since the earliest times, human beings have always needed oases of green escape – a relationship with nature. It is no wonder that in many religions Paradise is envisioned as a garden.

Landscaping of public places like highways, railway line, river banks *etc.* are to be prime importance for the benefit of people and to keep surroundings clean and neat.

Landscaping Highways

The landscaping of the national and state highways with trees is an important aspect of beautifying our countryside. Planting of trees on highways is necessary not only for the purpose of beautification but also for utility and necessity. The main purpose of roadside trees is to provide shade during the summer. For this purpose, evergreen trees with spreading crowns should be selected. For wider roads, double rows can be planted, with the outer rows having shade trees and the inner rows with flowering trees.

The planting of roadside trees started during the time of Emperor Asoka (268-231 *BC*). The Mughals also planted roadside trees. The roadside trees on the national highways not only provide shade but preferably also have some economic value. With this in view many of the highways have been planted with trees such as tamarind, mango, *Eugenia operculata* (syn *Syzygium operculatum*), *etc. Eugenia operculata* has one nuisance value as when its fruits ripe they drop on the road and make it dirty. The stain of this fruit is also difficult to remove from the clothes.

Neem (*Azadirachta indica*) (*Madhuca indica*), *sisso* (*Sisham*), and *Shorea robusta* (*Sal*) are roadside trees of economic value.

The highway trees should never be planted in mixed avenues, but only one species should be planted for a long distance of the road. For example, if neem trees are planted in pure avenue for a-long stretch, an oil extracting industry can be started on the roadside. Similarly, *Sal* yields valuable timber and its seeds yield an edible oil which is used as an ingredient in the manufacture of chocolates and other purposes. If a single species is planted in a pure avenue for miles together this looks more beautiful and gives a wavy appearance to the skyline. In such a case the management and gap-filling also become easier.

The trees should be planted 12 m apart in the row and at least 5 to 6 m away from the edge of the roads, so that they get enough space for spreading and do not interfere with the traffic. If a road is as wide as 30 m or more, double rows of trees should be planted, rows being spaced 10-12 m apart. The inner row may be of a flowering tree.

Trees with shallow root system such as *Millingtonia hortensis* and brittle wood as in the case of *Eugenia jambolana*, *Albizzia lebbek*, *Cassia siamea*, and Eucalyptus should never be planted on highways, as during storms they get uprooted or branches are broken and casualties may result on the unaware road users, *Neem* and tamarind can grow very well in dry localities. *Samanea saman* and *Dalbergia sisso* grow better in places having a rainfall of 100 cm or above. Banyans can be planted singly and a little away from the road at some distances, for its cool shade. *Albizzia procera* is a good roadside tree. *Polyalthia longifolia*, though not a tree of great economic value, is a very good shade tree and thus suitable for roadside planting. Thorny trees should not be planted along roadside as the falling thorns may damage the tyres of vehicles. Shrubbery borders with suitable shrubs can be maintained along the highways. This will improve the scenery.

Method of Planting

Mixed Plantation

Planting with different varieties of trees in a mixed avenue against the planting of a single species. This has got a couple of advantages. The first is that the different plants flower and fruit at various seasons thus enhancing the aesthetic view for a longer time of the year. The other advantage is that this planting avoids monotony.

Group Planting

A group of 3 to 4 or more trees are planted at specified intervals instead of planting in avenue.

Landscaping Railway Stations and Railway Line

One important aspect of bio-aesthetic planning is to landscape public places on a priority basis compared to private places. For this specific reason, the railway station and the railway lines should attract attention at the very outset for landscape gardening. The railway station is the first touching point for a visitor to the town. A well-kept and well-planted railway platform gives a visitor or a passer by the first impression about the town. It should be a social obligation on the part of our railway authorities to keep the platforms planted with beautiful trees. Trees offer the passengers a resting place under the hot sun, while waiting for the train. Concrete seats or benches could be constructed around the trunk or under the canopy for the benefit of the commuters.

Railway Stations

Besides flowering and foliage trees, the railway authorities can also improve and beautify the platforms with tubs and troughs planted with palms and other attractive plants such as bougainvilleas. Even hanging baskets can be displayed near the booking office or on the pillars of resting sheds and in similar other places.

One more aspect of why the railway platforms should be beautified with trees is that many more people pass through a railway station compared to those who visit a public park. Therefore, besides beautifying the area it will be possible to bring home the importance of bio-aesthetic planning to a large proportion of the population by landscaping a railway platform.

The railway stations are landscaped with avenues of such flowering beauties as *Cassia fistula (amaltas), Cassia nodosa, Peltochorum ferrugineum, Gulmohar, etc.* the tourist will carry back pleasant memories from India.

Railway Line

It will be a little hard task to landscape the vast stretches of railway lines compared to landscaping the platforms, especially in the drier tracts of the country. Fortunately, in India we have got beautiful flowering trees such as *Butea monosperma, Cassia fistula, Erythropsis colorata, etc.,* which can withstand considerable drought conditions.

The landscaping of railway lines poses some problems, the basic being watering. This can be partly overcome by planting drought-resistant trees during the rains. Plants should be deep-rooted and non-spreading. The trees are to be planted at a specified distance from the tracks as per railway regulations. These plants, besides breaking the monotony and drabness of the landscape, will offer shade to the gang workers.

The innumerable railway level-crossing are the places, which can be landscaped with much ease than the railway line, as the gate-man will be there to look after the plants. The gate-men who live there in the houses provided for them can be asked to plant a row of a few flowering trees on either side of the lines on both sides of the gate or in a small group-near the gate. The beauty of such trees will not only be enjoyed by the railway passengers but also by the people who pass by the road or wait for the train to pass.

The following trees are recommended for planting on railway platforms and lines.

Ornamental

Albizzia procera, Bauhinia variegata, Cassia fistula, C. javanica, C. nodosa, Delonix regia, Gliricidia maculate, Jacaranda mimosifolia, Lagerstroemia spp, Michelia champaka, Peltophorum ferrugineum, Polyalthia longifolia and Saraca indica.

Economic

Anacardium occidentale, Averrhoa carambola, Dalbergia sisso, Mangifera indica, Melia azedarach, Shorea robusta, Swietenia mahagoni, Tamarindus indica, Tectona grandis, Terminalia arjuna and *catappa.*

Landscaping along Banks of Rivers and Canals

The banks of the rivers and canals passing through towns and villages are well-suited for landscaping. The plants themselves will be objects of beauty and their reflection on the water surface is an additional attraction. The moisture-loving trees will do better along the water-front compared to others. In India, the rivers Yamuna, Ganges, Kauveri *etc.* are regarded as sacred and on the banks of these rivers are situated many old Hindu temples and *ghats*. The banks along these places should be planted with flowering trees, especially the sacred trees such as *Kadamba* (*Anthocephalus cadamba*) and *Asoka* (*Saraca indica*) which are associated with Lord Krishna and Godess Sita respectively.

The bank of the river Hoogly on the Kolkata side has been beautifully landscaped by the Kolkata port commissioners with shrubs and trees and has become a place for recreation for the citizens of the metropolis who can breathe fresh air away from the congested city. Besides, beautification, planting of trees along banks of rivers and canals help soil conservation also.

The dam sites which generally look drab should be converted into a place of beauty by landscaping with such beautiful trees as *Cassia nodosa, C. javanica, Gulmohar etc.* A garden or park can also be planned here, if space permits. The Brindavan Gardens in Mysore constructed below-a-dam site has become a place of great tourist attraction.

River banks near places of historic importance, such as Taj Mahal at on the bank of Yamuna, should also be landscaped with beautiful trees. The following flowering trees are recommended for planting along the banks of rivers and canals.

Amherstia nobilis, Anthocephalus cadamba, Barringtonia acutangula, Bauhinia variegata, Browneas, Cassia fistula, C. javanica, C. marginata, C. nodosa, Delonix regia,

Largerstroemia flos-reginae, L. thorelli, Melia azedarach ()ersian Lilac), *Peltophorum ferrugineum, Samanea saman,* and *Saraca indica.*

Landscaping City, Town and Countryside

In India most of the old cities and towns are unplanned without any consideration given to landscaping with trees and plants and as a result they look nothing but like brick and concrete jungles. The great architect Corbusier says that unless the conditions of nature are re-established in man's life, he cannot be healthy in body and spirit. The vast majorities of our population in the congested cities are cramped inside the four walls of their dwellings and are constantly injected with the fumes of petrol and other polluting agents.

Our towns and cities can be made more livable, healthy and beautiful and resorting to bio-aesthetic planning.

- ✰ This can be achieved by planting roadside trees and establishing parks planted with green plants.
- ✰ In the old congested cities this can be achieved by planning garden suburbs. Garden suburbs are nothing but satellite townships developed among parks and avenues.
- ✰ The cities can further be beautified by accommodating the slum dwellers in multi-storey buildings and utilizing the surplus land thus obtained for developing parks.
- ✰ The planning of new towns poses no problems as this can be planned in advance even before construction starts.

In a tropical country like India, the planting of roadside avenues are not only important for beautification, but also from utility point of view.

- ✰ Trees provide cool shade which is so much needed in the long hot summer.
- ✰ Trees also help in reducing air pollution,
- ✰ Act as wind break, and
- ✰ Cut down noise.
- ✰ Parks are places of relaxation,
- ✰ Entertainment, and
- ✰ Fresh air in an otherwise congested city.

Selection of trees for cities and towns with main criteria should be beauty and shade.

- ✰ The broad roads in the cities should be planted with double rows of trees; the outer rows should consist of shade trees, so as to provide shade to the footpath users and the inner row consisting of flowering trees adding beauty.

- M.S. Randhawa (ICS, the then President of ICAR) suggested long back that wide roads in the cities and towns should have two lanes on each side, one for fate-moving vehicles and the other for slow-moving vehicles flanked by footpaths. Each lane should be separated by a patch of land planted with grass and shrubs, while the outer rows are planted with double rows of flowering and shade trees.
- Planting the roads in a town or a city is a difficult proposition and this should be done in coordination with the electricity, telephone, and sewerage departments.
- The tree should not interfere with the telephone or electric lines of the underground sewers.
- Tall trees (*Eucalyptus, Araucaria, Millingtonia hortensis*) and trees with spreading habit (banyan, *Cedrus deodara, Ficus benjamina*) are not suitable for city or town roads.
- The tropical flowering trees are generally deciduous in habit and flower in leafless condition, which may be at a time when shade is needed to the maximum.The solution is, wherever feasible, to have an outer row of small shade trees such as *Ficus infectoria, Putranjiva roxburghii,* Silver oak, *Mimusops elengi etc.,* and inner row of flowering trees. The trees in either the rows, or when there is only a single row, should be planted in pure avenues *i.e.,* with one kind of tree only.

In many cities a piece of land is left out at the intersection of roads as a safeguard against accidents. These plots should be planted with grass and shrubs. One more novel way of beautifying the city roads is to train creepers on iron structures at regular intervals on foot paths. This has been done with *bougainvilleas* in cities such as New Delhi and Baroda.

Landscaping Country Side

The planting of trees in the countryside is done on a completely different criterion. Here more emphasis should be given on economic consideration and utility. The trees planted should provide the villager either with fuel, timber, fruit, or fodder.

- *Babul* is a common tree in the village, which is a cheap source of fuel and is used for the manufacture of wheel of bullock-carts. The bark of this tree is used for tanning leather.
- *Desi* (seedling) mango and jackfruit trees also yield timber for making doors and windows and other household articles such as charpais, benches, *etc.*
- *Dalbergia sisso* is also a good source of timber and fuel.
- *Sal* trees are good for both fuel and timber.
- Some minor fruit trees should be planted along the country road in open spaces. This will not only provide shade but will yield valuable fruits for the villagers.

- ☆ Jackfruit is an important fruit tree for arid regions.
- ☆ The toddy or palmyra palm (*Borassus flabellifer*) is an important tree, which yields a minor edible fruit but the leaves are used extensively for thatching roofs of dwellings.
- ☆ Both date and palmyra palms look beautiful when planted in rows along country roads or on the borders of cultivated fields or when planted in informal groups.
- ☆ *Mahua* and large-fruited *jamuns* (*Syzygium cumini*) can also be planted.
- ☆ The foliage plants yield valuable fodder for the cattle and goats, *babul, Kachnar* (*Bauhinia*), *neem,* and *ber* (*Zizyphus* spp.) *ber also* produces edible fruits.

However, ornamental trees should also be planted near the *Panchayet,* schools, churches, mosques, temples and *Gurudwaras* and along the field boundaries and near the village well or pond.

Landscaping a Small Home Ground

There are many people who think that landscape gardening relates to only gardening in large public parks or palaces of the rich. Landscaping as it is done for larger estates or public parks can also be implemented in a tasteful and artistic way for a small home ground, though on a smaller scale. The simplest definition of small, as suggested by some authors quite appropriately, is an area which can be effectively managed and maintained physically as well as financially by the owner and his family with occasional hired labour for such hard work as digging, mowing, and shearing of hedges. Here, ways will be suggested for landscaping only small residential houses. For larger estates, a combination of landscaping effects suggested for parks and home landscaping may be followed.

Basic Guidelines for a Home Landscape

The personal preference plays a considerable role in developing a home garden. The home including its surroundings should be an outward expression of the inner personality and individuality of the owner. It is advisable to think a lot before even a single digging work starts.

Basic Principles

Before actually drawing the master-plan the following points should be kept in mind in home landscaping.

(a) ***Background***: The background in a garden, whether a wall, tall trees or a hedge should be neutral in nature; that is to say this should not become a distracting feature over the main features of the garden.

(b) ***Contrast:*** The design should be such that it should break monotony. To achieve this, variation in form, texture, or colour has to be brought in.

(c) ***Balance or proportion:*** A balance has to be maintained between different components (masses, forms, colour, *etc.*) of a garden. Overcrowding of plants or other garden features should be avoided.

(d) ***Open centre:*** The central area of the garden should be left out of any items of major interest. The best way to achieve this is to have a lawn, which also gives an effect of largeness to the property. A specimen shrub in the centre of the lawn is unsuitable as this counters the principle of spaciousness, but a tree branching at higher levels from the ground could be planted.

(e) ***Repetition:*** The repetition or duplicating some features of a garden helps achieve rhythm, balance and unity. In a formal garden, generally the same feature is repeated. But for an informal design this need not be so. Here one may repeat the colour tone without disturbing the texture, form, or quantity. If there is a circular path this can be repeated by having two or three consecutive circular shaped beds of annual flowers, hedges, and shrubbery border. Thus, though the shape is repeated, the variation in texture, colour and form ensure that the design does not look monotonous.

(f) ***Rhythm:*** A landscape designer should have an artistic sense to understand how to bring in rhythm in the design. Arranging the different elements haphazardly, without harmony, does not enhance beauty. Harmonious lines, often artistically curved, bring in rhythm to the landscape. A group of shrubs in front of a rockery breaks the rhythm. Repetition of certain elements, such as form, enhances the rhythm.

(g) ***Variety:*** To break the monotony in a garden, variety is essential. This is achieved by contrast of colour, form, and texture.

Besides these, design should be simple, easy to maintain and provide comfort for inmates.

Making a Plan

If the garden area is sufficiently large, this can be divided into three areas.

(1) ***Approach or Public area:*** This is the area from the street side extending to the entrance of the house. The approach area should not be overcrowded with large trees. It is better to have doorway or "foundation" plantings with low growing shrubs and evergreens.

Big trees, if space permits, can go in the backyard but should not be overcrowded in the front. But a few low-growing trees can be accommodated at the appropriate places as next to entrance, if space is available or somewhere in the front lawn. An open spacious lawn with some annuals (zinnias, salvias and petunias) or herbaceous perennials (chrysanthemum, canna and *Impatiens* in shade) can be planned in addition to the foundation plantings.

(2) ***Work or Service area:*** Wherever feasible this and the living area should be situated at the back of the house as these need privacy. This area includes the kitchen garden, compost bin, nursery, tool shed and garage.

(3) ***Private Garden area or Living area:*** In the western countries, this is generally termed as the outdoor living area, where people sit out in the winter to enjoy the sun or rest in the summer under an arbour or shade of tree. This area should be easily approachable and visible from the living (drawing-room) or dining-room, screened from unsightly objects and for privacy. In the western countries people prefer a terrace and this is the place where it should come. There should be some shaded sitting spot such as a tree or arbour with garden benches. A wide stretch of lawn with shrub border or few annuals beds or a rose garden can also be included in this section. A tennis court or a play area has to be included here, if there is enough room.

Many people advise not to include any pool or formal rock garden or the kind in a home garden. But there is no harm, if a formal or informal lily pool can fit in with the overall design, with or without a fountain or a rock garden. A statue or sun dial can also be well fitted in some spacious compounds.

A doorway near the house needs special attention as this is the place which receives maximum attention from a visitor. Depending upon the approach a doorway can be planted informally, formally, or in a semi-informal pattern. It can be arranged with a garden-type design consisting of an ornamental shade or flowering tree perennial and annual flowers, climbing roses, some bulbs such as *Zephyranthes, Amaryllis,* and daffodils (for temperate regions). A bed of roses can also be a spot of beauty provided it receives the morning sun. Symmetrical plants with pyramidal form such as *Thuja, Juniperus chinensis,* and *Cupressus macrocarpa* are preferred by many near the doorway for a formal treatment.

Trees Suitable for Small Gardens

Bauhinias in different species are quite suitable. Bottle brush is suitable for many situations. *Tecoma argentea,* Cassia *fistula,* and *Cassia spectabilis,* Cherries, (*Prunus sargentii*), Weeping willow (*Salix babylonica*) and *S. purpurea* var. *pendula* are also very ornamental. Some shrubs *Ixora singaporensis, Mussaenda philippica, Azalea etc.*

Landscaping a Country Home

A villager in India may not need a sophisticated garden. However, a countryman will need as much privacy as a city dweller. A village home has to be planned with more utility items. A villager would like to grow more vegetables and fruit for his family consumption and consequently more area should be earmarked for this purpose. But few shade trees and some area reserved for children's palygorund is definitely needed. Some utility flowering trees such as *Michelia champaka, Plumeria acutifolia* and shrubs such as *Hibiscus rosa-sinensis, Tabernaemontana coronaria, Barleria, Crossandra,* and jasmines yielding flowers for worshipping and hair decoration should be included for planting.

The common flowering annuals such as marigold, zinnia, balsam, and sunflower can be grown for beauty and cut-flowers for various purposes.

Landscaping Cemeteries and Burning Ghats

The landscaping of cemeteries and burning *ghats* may sound paradoxical under Indian conditions. This is a country where a large number of people do not even get the minimum amount of food to keep them alive during their life-time, so the idea of having a garden around their tombs after death may sound ridiculous at the first thought. But there is a need for this also, not only from the point of peace, tranquility, and beauty, but also to fight pollution and provide shade. Whether the body is buried or burnt in an ugly surrounding or a beautiful landscape matters nothing to the departed person (unless, of course, we believe in life after death), but it certainly has some sobering effect on the sorrow-laden hearts of the near and dear ones who attend the funeral. While bidding final farewell one would definitely like the last resting place of one's dearest in a quiet, peaceful surrounding. For this reason also, a cemetery needs to be landscaped with trees, shrubs, and grass.

The cemetery is sub-divided into several sections and each section is made accessible by providing driveways at a distance of 50-100 m depending upon the size of the place. In small places of 3-4 hectares no driveway is needed and the walks in such cemetery may be left in grass only. Most of the area in the cemetery should be left under grass with few trees grouped here and there for immediate effect. More trees, especially the evergreen types, are planted along the boundaries. Some flowering trees *etc.*, of course, selected to bring a bright and cheerful effect. The buildings should be modest in appearance and be planted with shrubbery and vines.

Under Indian conditions also it is possible to keep the cemeteries in a park-like fashion without much elaborate arrangements. The basis will be the same as stated above with emphasis on modesty and sobriety. In India many cemeteries have been planted with trees mainly for the purpose of shade and to create some formal effect. Very often there will be some shade-trees such as seedling mango, banyan, *neem, etc.* and the roads are lined with *Polyalthia longifolia* var, *pendula, Plumeria acutifolia* may also be planted in burial grounds, which flowers freely under most Indian conditions.

The burning *ghats* in India present a picture of horror and sorrow, which can definitely be improved upon by proper landscaping. It is not possible to have a formal garden with grass, flower beds, *etc.* in a conventional burning *ghat,* for obvious reason, but the picture can be changed by planting in groups, some shade and flowering trees. In most cases these *ghats* are located near water tanks, ponds or rivers. The ponds can be planted with water-lilies and lotus while the banks can be beautified by planting shade and flowering trees. In modern electric crematoriums it is possible to layout a formal or an informal garden around it with important features such as trees shrubbery, flower beds, lawns, *etc.*

The "Towers of Silence" of the Parsi community afford good scope for gardening. Since these towers have long stretches of ground all around them, a nice garden with lawn, shrubbery, and flowering trees along the periphery, can be laid out. For instance, the Tower of Silence near Bangalore has a long avenue of jacarandas which, when in bloom, present wonderful scenery.

Chapter 20

Planning for Gardening of Public Places

The places of historic importance such as tomb, forts, historic monuments *etc.*, can be laid out with vast stretches of lawns, large ponds, canna beds, shade and flowering trees *etc.*, keep in view that the planting should not over-shadow the monument. The trees should be selected depending upon the climate of the region. In dry area, the approach roads to the historic spot can be planted with drought withstanding flowering trees such as *Erythrina indica*.

Temples, Gurudwaras, Mosques, Churches

Religious building are the places of worship. In such places, the scope is restricted especially in large cities because of space problem. But in villages and towns, the places of worships form good scope for bio-aesthetic planning. It is important to have a garden with the optimum type of flowering plants.

Buddhist Temples

The association of *Plumeria alba* is so common with Buddhist temples that it is commonly called as 'Temple tree' or 'Pagoda tree'.

Hindu Temple

Shrubs such as jasmines, crossandra, barleria *etc.*, are quite useful in a Hindu temple. Seasonal flowers such as marigold and small flowering chrysanthemums (yellow flowering type) can also be planted around Hindu temples. Generally, there will be come water tank in the vicinity of a Hindu temple. This should be planted with water lilies and lotus and on the banks moisture loving trees may be planted. Some sweet scented flowering trees such as *Michelia champaka* should be planted around the temple to create an atmosphere of serenity and sanctity. There should be enough open space in the front to the devotees to assemble there under the shade of trees. A tree of *Saraca indica* is another sacred tree which should find a place in a Hindu temple.

Church

In **Church places**, foundation planting with shrubbery is quite useful. Potted plants can also be arranged near the portico. There is scope for displaying hanging baskets especially for Gothic type buildings.

In front of **mosques,** Mughal type gardens can be laid out with stress on formal water pools fitted with fountains.

Planning for Layout of Public Buildings

The government and private offices, courts, auditoria, cinemas, hotel and travelers bungalows fall under the group of public buildings. If there is paucity of space, potted plants are used to decorate the entrance and the corridors. But where space is available, a lawn should be laid with a few flower beds and possibly some shrub border may be added. The entrance and exit roads may be lined with flowering trees. Majestic looking non spreading large trees will be the right choice for skyscrapers.

Some flowering climbers may be trained over the portico. If the compound is properly planted with a few shade and flowering trees and a nice lawn, the people will find a resting place. A miniature garden with lawn, flower-beds, shrubbery, lily pool, fountain and a few specimen trees can be planted in Travelers' Bungalow garden. Hotel buildings should also have gardens of the same style if space is available. Fountains fitted with coloured light can also be added. Sufficient parking space should also be provided.

Garden in Educational Institutions

In the periphery of the School Campus, along the rear and wings, a thick beet of large shady trees should be planted with medium sized flowering trees for beauty. A flower parade can be created along the periphery. Eucalyptus, silver oak and *Polyanthia longifolia* are suitable for peripheral planting. Where are electric wires limit the choice of avenue trees, small flowering trees for instance *Cochlospemum gossypium, Callistemon lanceolatus, Bauninia variegata and Tabubia argentea* can be planted *Cassia fistula, C. nodosa, Gulmohar, Tabubia argentea, Erythrina indica, Lagerstroemia flos-reginae* and *Bauhinia variegata* are suitable for planting in the front row of the border planting. Border planting of shrubbery on large ground or at the back of the school campus serves useful purpose of filling the gaps between the trees and lawns. Small paths can be planted with shrubs. Shrub borders around playgrounds are very effective.

The foundation planting can also be undertaken with evergreen dwarf and trailing shrubs. A playground can be planted with lawn. A bougainvillea creeps, trained over the wall of the building or *Bignonia venusta* supported against a wall looks beautiful. Creepers such as *Ficus repen, Ficus puemilla, Campsis radicans* (*Syn. Tecoma radicans*) can be trained over some stone or brick wall or pillar. A bird bath provided amidst the trees will be educative to the students.

Gardening in Factories

In factories such as cement, steel, fertilizers *etc.*, which emit a lot of dust, smoke and harmful chemicals, and comparatively hardy plants, are to be selected. For neat factories such as a plywood factory and a fruit-processing plant, which emit less dust and other polluting materials, a wider range of plant which emits less dust and other polluting materials can be used.

The primary aim in a factory garden is to plant trees to arrest the drifting dust and smoke and to cut down noise. Tall and hardy trees such is *Casuarina equisetifolia, Eucalyptus, Polyalthia longifolia* and silver oak should be planted all round or in the direction of the winds to stop the spread of dust and smoke. In a large factory a buffer zone may be created by afforestation between the factory and its residential colony. Afforestation can be done with hardy ornamentals such as *Acacia auriculiformis, Casuarina equisetifolia, Dulbergia sisso* and some other shade trees. A factory can also be beautiful with rockeries, statues, water pools or lakes, fountains *etc.* Bougainvillea should be used freely to beautify a factory area. This may be planted in rows along all the roads of the factory spaced at 3-5m and trained as half standards. Canna a hardy plant is suitable for planting in beds or groups in a factory area. Shrubberies consisting of hardy shrubs also beautify factories. Lawns add beauty and cut down dust.

Landscaping at Bus Terminal and Airport

Now-a-days, with the increase in road traffic many state governments are constructing large bus terminals and bus stations, but except in a few States such as Haryana these stations consist of nothing but concrete and tar. The bus terminals should be beautified on the lines of railways stations.

Airports should also be beautified by planting ornamental trees, lawns, flower beds and displaying plants in tubs and troughs. Fortunately, many of the airports in India are quite nicely landscaped, but there is some scope to improve them.

Lawns

Low maintenance, drought resistant turf grasses are to be used in place of traditional lawn/turf grass.

Low or Slow Growing

Turf grass species are to grow at a rate that does not require excessive mowing, *i.e.* more than twice a month during the growing season or no more than six times a year or the mature height of the species does not exceed the recommended mow height.

Drought Tolerant

Turf grass species are to require no additional irrigation except during establishment. The species must be suitable to Chicago's climate (USDA Zone 5) and precipitation ranges. Kentucky Bluegrass (*Poa pratensis*) varieties are not acceptable.

Seed Mixes

Readily available proprietary or other agency-specified seed mixtures are to be used whenever possible. It is recommended that seed mixtures consist of a variety of acceptable turf grass species that promote diversity and thereby minimize susceptibility to disease and to promote a longer growing season by utilizing complimentary cool-season and warm-season grass species where possible. An annual nurse crop may be added to the seed mix to aid establishment of the turf.

Maintenance

A maintenance plan for turf grasses should be devised and implemented that at a minimum addresses the following maintenance issues:

Mowing

All turf grass areas must be maintained at a height of 5 to 8 inches (Source: Cleary, E.C. and R.A. Dolbeer. July 2005. "Wildlife Hazard Management at Airports", FAA and USDA, 2nd ed., Appendix O). This recommended mowing height reduces the attraction of geese, gulls, and crows and at the same time does not promote excessive cover for small mammals that may attract large raptors. In addition, the mowing frequency should be reduced as much as possible to limit the disturbance of insect populations that may attract wildlife in the mowed areas.

Irrigation

No additional irrigation is to be provided beyond what is required for initial establishment.

Fertilization

Beyond initial establishment, fertilizer should be used sparingly on native turf grasses and in some cases eliminated all together as it is detrimental to some species and also because it exacerbates weed problems. Periodic fertilization for native, low-maintenance turf should only occur every other year and at half the recommended application rate for typical commercial lawn fertilizers.

Landscaping City Parks

In city there may be parks of several sizes from very large to medium size and also squares or small gardens are generally found at street intersections. The small gardens or squares are planted with a view to relieving the eyes of the people passing by them or for a short resting period for shoes who care to use them. Therefore, these may be planted with a patch of grass, few flower beds, one or two shade or flowering trees or a group of shrubs and trees. The medium to large parks are meant for a place of recreation and these are considered as lungs of the cities. These should be a place of beauty as well as utility.

Good flowering and shade trees should be planted in groups or singly in some corners or other suitable places for creating beauty as well as a place for resting. Garden benches should be constructed at regular intervals especially under the shade of the trees. Few interesting and rare shrubs should also be included. Besides these, some garden adornments such as statues and fountains can also be planned in appropriate parts of such parks.

City parks may be called as pleasure grounds which have large reserve areas for playing games, and often this is the main feature of these parks. A restricted swimming pool is also often a feature of a pleasure ground. If it is meant for the children, features such as swings, see-saw, sliding chute, merry-go-round, *etc.*, should form part of the park. Due to hard usage it is almost impossible to maintain grass area within this park. Some trees and shrubs are planted aesthetically to keep the place pleasing to the eyes.

Ornamental Trees Recommended for Town Road

Ornamental Shade Trees

Anthocephalus cadamba, Ficus infectoria, Melia azadirachta, Polyalthia longifolia, Putranjiva roxburghii, Swietenia mahagoni, Tamarindus indica.

Flowering Trees

Bauhinia purpurea, B. variegata, Cassia fistula, C. javanica, C. marginata, C. nodosa, Gliricidia maculate, Jacaranda mimosaefolia, Lagerstroemia flos-reginae, Peltophorum ferrugineum, Poinciana (Delonix) regia, Saraca indica, and Spathodea campanulata

Chapter 21

Designing of Greenhouse etc.

India has a very long tradition of floriculture. References to flowers and gardens are found in ancient Sanskrit classics. The offering and exchange of flowers on all social occasions, in places of worship and their use for adornment of hair by women and for home decoration have become an integral part of human living. With changing life-styles urban areas, floriculture has assumed commercial status in recent times.

Greenhouse is an artificial constructed shade and covered structures of plastic film, which allow the solar radiation to pass through but traps the thermal radiation emitted by plants inside and thereby provide favourable climatic conditions for plant growth. It is the ultra-mode device used for controlling temperature, humidity, light intensity, CO_2 level inside. Greenhouse is a framed or inflated structure covered with transparent or translucent material large enough to grow crops under partial or fully controlled environmental conditions to get optimum growth, productivity and quality

Points to be Remembered for Construction of Greenhouse

1. Construction of greenhouse depends on the purpose, type of crop, crop growth, quality requirements, market destination, demand, time of supply, quantity, type of business – retail or wholesale, cut flower production, planting material, seed production *etc.*

2. Topography, drainage, ground slope, soil condition, temperature, relative humidity, wind velocity and direction, rainfall, snow fall, irrigation facility, year round weather conditions *etc.*
3. Input availability, labour, equipments, transportation facilities, electricity/power supply *etc.*
4. Production area, sales, area, storage, post harvest handling area, area for expansion, expertise, marketing *etc.*
5. Economic requirement, feasibility, profitability *etc.*

Types of Greenhouse Structure Available

The greenhouse are classified or named depending upon the type of material used for construction, type of glazing used, shape and number of spans, environmental control system, purpose *etc.* There are based on the given points:

I. Number of Spans (Span – the distance between two gutters)

a. **Single span:** Also called detached type where only a single unit covering an area about 100 to 500m^2.

b. **Multi-span:** Also called ridge and furrow or gutter connected greenhouses where number of single span greenhouses is joined together. The ridge side of single span greenhouses is connected with gutters to able to drain the rainwater falling on the roof. The greenhouse area may be up to one hectare or more.

Single span or multi-span green houses may be constructed in Quonset or Gable type.

II. Shape of the Structure

a. **Quonset type:** Also called arch roofed or hoop shaped of the greenhouse is semicircular or arch shaped with medium to high sidewall, most commonly constructed type for single span or multi span greenhouses.

b. **Gable type:** Also called angular or triangle type, wherein the shape of the roof is in angular form with medium to high sidewalls. Most suitable for temperate region for easy sliding or snowfall during winter.

c. **Trussed type:** Similar to Quonset or Gable type but provided with additional structural unit called trusses to the roof to strengthen the load of the frame.

d. **Ground to ground or tunnel type:** Semicircular shaped roof touching the ground on either side without any sidewall or side screen for natural ventilation. Such structures are mostly used for propagation and rising plants with small stature.

e. **Lean to type:** Greenhouse is said to be lean to type if its one side especially northern side forms the sidewall of the building and the roof is leaned to only one side.

f. **Uneven span:** If the span is uneven and not symmetric about its long axis then the structure is termed uneven span.

III. Environmental Control System

1. **Low-cost greenhouse/polyhouse;**The low-cost polyhouse is a zero-energy chamber made of polythene sheet of 700 gauge supported on bamboos with 'sutli' and 'nails'. Its size depends on the purpose of its utilization and availability of space. Like the greenhouse, it has one opening kept *azar* for 1-2 hr during the day, especially in the morning to reduce the level of humidity inside. The temperature within polyhouse increases by 6-10°C more than outside. In UV-stabilized plastic film covered, pipe framed polyhouse, the day temperature is higher and night temperature lower than the outside. The solar radiations entering the polyhouse is 30-40 per cent lower than that reaching the soil surface outside.
2. **Medium-cost greenhouse/polyhouse:**With a slightly higher cost, a Quonset-shaped polyhouse (greenhouse) can be framed with GI pipe (class B) of 15 mm bore. This polyhouse has a single layer covering UV-stabilized polythene of 800 gauge. The exhaust fans are used for ventilation those are thermostatically controlled. Cooling pad is used for humidifying the air entering the polyhouse. The polyhouse frame and glazing material have a life span of about 20 years and 2 years respectively.
3. **Hi-tech greenhouse/polyhouse;**This type of greenhouse consists of a sensor, a comparator and an operator. The temperature, humidity and light are automatically controlled. These are indicated through sensor or signal-receiver. Sensor measures the variables, compare the measurement to a standard value and finally recommend to run the corresponding device. For example, temperature control system consists of temperature sensor, heating/cooling mechanism and thermostat-operated fan. Similarly, relative humidity is sensed through optical tagging devices. Boiler operation, irrigation and misting systems are operated under pressure sensing system. This modern structure is highly expensive, requiring qualified operators, maintenance, care and precautions.

IV. Utility

a. **Cold frames:** greenhouses used for hardening of seedlings in the spring season.

b. **Hot beds:** If the greenhouses are artificially heated, they are called hot beds. Heating is necessary in temperate regions where the temperature goes much below 0°C.

c. **Other types:** Greenhouses are also classified based on the use and purposes. It may be retail or a wholesale greenhouse, greenhouses for academic or research units, Public Park, instructional greenhouses *etc.*

Plates

Principles of Landscape Designs.

Propagation of Ornamental Plants.

Tissue Culture.

Layout of Shade Garden, Sunken and Vertical Gardens.

Desinging of Greenhouse, Conservatory and Lathhouse.

Layout of Marsh or Bog Garden.

Layout of Informal Gardens.

Layout of Roof Gardens.

Etymology

Badlands National Park,
South Dakota, USA.

Tropical Rainforest,
Fatu Hiva Island, Marquesas
Islands, French Polynesia.

Tundra in Siberia, Russia.

Taiga (Boreal Forest), Alaska, US.

Desert: The Rain Shadow Region
of Tirunelveli, India.

A Wetland: Viru Bog in
Lahemaa National Park in Estonia.

The Aletsch Glacier, the Largest Glacier in the Swiss Alps.

Large Fields of Modern Farmland, Dorset, England.

Autumn Landscape in Rybiniszki, Latvia, Watercolor by Stanisław Masłowski, 1902 (National Museum in Warsaw, Poland).

Kukle, Czech Republic.

Different Types of Landscape

Panorama of the Chaîne des Puys from Puy de Dôme in winter. Massif Central, France. An example of how past volcanic activity shaped a landscape.

Landscape Archaeology

Medieval Ridge and Furrow above Wood Stanway, Gloucestershire, England.

Cultural Landscape

The Batad Rice Terraces, The Rice Terraces of the Philippine Cordilleras, the first site to be included in the UNESCO World Heritage List cultural landscape category in 1995.

Stourhead Garden, Wiltshire, England.

Jichang Garden in Wuxi (1506–1521).

Landscape Architecture

Central Park, New York City, US, Designed by Frederick Law Olmsted.

Landscape and Literature

The Djabugay language group's mythical being, *Damarri*, transformed into a mountain range, is seen lying on his back above the Barron River Gorge, looking upwards to the skies, within north-east Australia's wet tropical forested landscape.

The Tetons and the Snake River (1942).

The Vale of Blackmore, the main setting for Thomas Hardy's novel *Tess of the d'Urbervilles*. Hambledon Hill towards Stourton Tower.

Salomon van Ruisdael, "*View of Deventer*" (1657).

Thomas Cole "The Course of Empire The Arcadian or Pastoral State", US, 1836.

Claude Lorrain, *Landscape with Apollo Guarding the Herds of Admetus and Mercury stealing them* (1645).

Albert Bierstadt, The Matterhorn (circa 1867).

Landscape with scene from the Odyssey, Rome, c. 60-40 BC.

Vincent van Gogh, *Wheat Fields at Auvers Under Clouded Sky* (1890).

Pablo Picasso, 1908, *Paysage aux deux figures* (Landscape with Two Figures).

Paul Nash, *Wire* (1918).

Bibliography

Anner, Leslie, 1989. *Handbook of Integrated Pest Management for Turf and Ornamentals*, Lewis Publishers, Washington.

Arora, J.S., 1998. *Introductory Ornamental Horticulture*, Kalyani Publishers, Ludhiana.

Bhattacharjee S.K. and L.C. De., 2003. *Advanced Commercial Floriculture*, Aavishkar Publishers, Jaipur.

Bhattacharjee S.K., L.C. De.2005. *Postharvest Technology of Flowers and Ornamental Plants*, Pointer Publishers, Jaipur.

Bose and Yadav, 1989. *Commercial Flowers*, Naya Prokash, Calcutta.

Bose, T.K., D. Mukherjee, 1977. *Gardening in India*, Oxford and IBH Publishing Co., Calcutta.

Bose, T.K., L.P. Yadav, P. Pal, P. Das and V.A. Parthasarathy, 2002. *Commercial Flowers*, Vol. 1 and Vol. 2, Naya Udyog, Kolkata.

Chadha, K.L., 2014. *Handbook of Horticulture*, ICAR, Ministry of Agriculture, New Delhi.

Das, S.N., 2004. *Growing Bulbous Ornamental Plants*, Agrotech Publishing Academy, Udaipur.

Dey, S.C., 2001. *Complete Home Gardening*, Agrobios, India.

Grewal, H.S., 1999. *Propagation of Ornamental Plants*, Kalyani Publishers, New Delhi.

John H. Madison, 1971. *Practical Turf Grass Management*. Van Nostrand Reinhold, New York.

Malcolin Hillier, 1995. *Container Gardening*, DK Publishing (Dorling Kindersley),

Pal, B.P., 1991. *The Rose in India*, ICAR Publication, New Delhi.

Peter chan, 1989. *Bonsai*, Dorset Books,

Phillips, Rose and Rix, Martyr. *The Ultimate Guide to Roses.*

Prasad, S. and U. Kumar, 2001. *Greenhouse Management for Horticultural Crops*, Agrobios, India.

Randhawa, G.S. and A. Mukhopadhyaya, 1986. *Floriculture in India*, Allied publishers Pvt. Limited, New Delhi

Roy A Larson, 1992. *Introduction to Floriculture*, Academic Press, Inc. A Division of Harcourt Brace and Company, California.

Salunkhe, D. K., Bhatt, Desai, 1990. *Postharvest Biotechnology of Flowers and Ornamental Plants*, Naya Prokash, Calcutta.

Surendra Prasad Updesh Kumar, 1998. *Commercial Floriculture*, Agro Botanical Publishers, India.

Swarup, Vishnu, 2002. *Inoor Gardening*. ICAR Publication, New Delhi.

Tiwari, G.N. and R.K. Goyal. 1998. *Greenhouse Technology*, Narosa publishing house: New Delhi,

Trivedi, P.P. 2004. *Home Gardening*. ICAR Publication, New Delhi.

Vargas, J.M, 1994. *Management of Turfgrass Diseases* – II Edn, Lewis Publishers, Washington.

Index